A PENCHANT FOR PENSIONS

A GUIDE TO ACTUARIAL VALUATIONS FOR PUBLIC PENSION FUNDS

LESLIE L. THOMPSON, FSA, FCA, EA, MAAA
PAMELA M. FEELY, CPA, MBA, AF

A Penchant for Pensions
by Leslie L. Thompson, FSA, FCA, EA, MAAA and
Pamela M. Feely, CPA, MBA, AF

Published by

Campaign Finance Guides, LLC

Cover and interior layout by Nick Zelinger, NZ Graphics

ISBN: 978-0-9973173-2-9
LCCN: 2018950033

First Edition

Printed in the USA

Authors' Notes

Many have joined us on this journey to take the actuarial valuation process out of the "black box." Now, public sector pension trustees have a reference guide that provides useful and meaningful information decoding the actuarial valuation process.

Pam Feely, co-author, was the original energy behind starting and completing this book. Without her knowledge of how to write, edit, and publish a book this endeavor would not have reached completion. Without her constant encouragement this book may have died a slow death.

The authors wish to thank Mike Daniels for his expert advice and his navigational skills from the start of the book to its final production. Janet Arrowood's editing helped us to better communicate the technical and tangled concepts surrounding actuarial systems. Janet's patience and thoroughness is gratefully acknowledged. Nick Zelinger's artistic assistance created a more readable technical work.

Brian Murphy, FSA, FCA, EA, MAAA, PhD provided many hours and invaluable technical oversight. Without his technical expertise some of the issues would not be presented nearly as clearly or precisely.

Finally, the authors wish to thank Gabriel, Roeder, Smith and Company. To be able to partner with a firm so dedicated to the public sector retirement world has been of immeasurable help. The authors gratefully acknowledge the financial support provided by Gabriel, Roeder, Smith and Company in underwriting this project.

Contents

About Gabriel, Roeder, Smith & Company

Gabriel, Roeder, Smith & Company (GRS) generously contributed to the costs for producing this book. The authors gratefully acknowledge their contribution to the editing, artistry and publication of this book.

GRS is a national actuarial and benefit consulting firm that brings clients innovative solutions for pension and retiree medical actuarial services. In 1938, GRS' founders dedicated their lives to ensuring retirement security in the United States. GRS continues to build upon this vision by helping its clients develop and maintain fiscally sustainable benefit programs that preserve financial security for millions of Americans. Each year, GRS works with well over a thousand public sector clients across the country. It serves more public pension clients than any other firm in the industry. This book represents GRS' commitment to making retirement security a reality for future generations of employees and retirees.

GRS is an employee-owned private company with its resources fully dedicated to serving the public sector. The Company's main offices are located in Detroit, Ft. Lauderdale, Dallas, Chicago, Denver, and Minneapolis.

GRS is an independent corporation and is unique in the actuarial industry due to the focus on providing actuarial and related retirement consulting services solely to the public sector. The independence ensures that GRS can continue to focus on the public sector. For more than 80 years GRS has provided actuarial consulting services on pensions, retiree medical and health care plans to states, cities, counties, public safety, special districts and other metropolitan agencies. GRS has spoken on behalf of their clients to state legislatures, commissions, city councils and other legislative bodies.

Overall GRS client relationships span over three million public sector employees and retirees. GRS's broad client base includes more than 1,000 public sector entities, from large state-wide systems to the local volunteer firefighter plans. More than 10,000 actuarial valuations are produced annually.

GRS participates on a national scale, serving on the Boards and committees of well-known national organizations such as the National Association of State Retirement Administrators, the National Conference of Public Employee Retirement Systems, the National Council on Teacher Retirement and the Government Finance Officers Association. GRS consultants can be seen participating at many local and regional organizations.

GRS's singular focus on the public sector has led to the development of actuarial valuation and modeling software that is uniquely responsive to the needs of public sector clients. Modeling the future and assessing its various risks is a key component to their actuarial and consulting relationships. GRS's software assists clients in understanding the potential future outcomes for their plan while also modeling impacts to budgets and long term financial commitments.

GRS remains committed to education for its clients. GRS hopes that this book will serve as one more opportunity to enhance our clients decision making capabilities in order to provide secure retirement for their clients.

Further information on GRS can be found at www.grsconsulting.com

PART I

INTRODUCTION

Introduction

OUR WELCOME TO THE READER

Welcome to the world of actuarial science! This book is a guide to assist you through the maze of decisions you face as trustees.

We have written this guide to assist trustees, from newly appointed with little-to-no actuarial or financial background, through the most experienced trustees, to gain a firmer grasp of the nuances and impacts of their vital roles.

We trust this guide leads you, as trustees, to the optimal outcome for your pension fund. Your fiduciary duty is continually challenged and evolving as you seek to balance competing obligations. You may not have a crystal ball, but you do have ...

A PENCHANT FOR PENSIONS

And this book will help you make your best choices by drawing on the information we provide.

1

The Defined Benefit Pension Plan

THE BENEFIT PROMISE

A defined benefit pension plan promises a regular benefit amount at a member's retirement age. Rarely are payments decreased. Defined benefit plans are prominent in the public sector and currently not in favor in the private sector.

This section of our guide focuses on defined benefit plans as found in the public sector. Note that some of these plans are 100% employer funded, while others are funded with a combination of employee and employer contributions. For purposes of clarity, employees are referred to as members once they are eligible for participation in the defined benefit plan and retirees once they begin receiving payments under the plan.

How are plan benefits calculated? There are two methods. The benefit may be a flat dollar amount. For example, a plan might promise $300 per month after the member has worked for 20 years under the terms of the plan. Or, a plan might promise $10 per month per year of service. Many plans base the benefit promise on the member's final average compensation. These formulas use a multiplier such as "1.5%" of the member's final average compensation for each year of service. Table 1 provides an example of this calculation.

Table 1: Plan Benefit Calculation

Compensation-three years ago	$40,000
Compensation-two years ago	$42,000
Compensation-one year ago	$45,000
Final three-year average	$42,333
Years of credited service	20
Annual benefit amount payable at normal retirement age (1.5% multiplier * $42,333*20)	$12,699

These benefits are payable from retirement until death. Members may choose a payment option that continues the benefit to their spouse upon the member's death.

Many people contribute to Social Security during their working careers. Social Security is a defined benefit plan. The amount promised is a recurring dollar amount, payable from initial election of payments until the member's death. Each Social Security beneficiary's monthly amount depends on their earnings history. However, some public employees and their employers do not contribute to Social Security. When those public employees retire they are not eligible to collect Social Security.

Historically, both private and public sector employers maintained defined benefit plans. A member's expenses at retirement were anticipated to be regular, recurring, and generally well-defined. The defined benefit plan was the most reasonable way to help "match" those expenses. A recurring monthly payment allowed a member to retire with a sense of economic security.

In the past, employees tended to work for the same employer their entire careers. Job-hopping was frowned upon. In exchange for loyalty, employers provided the opportunity for a timely and affordable retirement. Employers recognized the need to allow older employees to transition out of employment. These employers also recognized creating a path to retirement provided advancement opportunities for younger employees.

Employers also recognized that a stagnating workforce may create an increase in expenses. Employees working longer than expected create additional expenses for a company's bottom line. For example, these longer service employees will have higher salaries, higher health care costs, and higher pension plan contributions. Limited opportunities for advancement cause younger workers to move on to other organizations. This phenomenon also impacts local, state, and federal governments.

FUNDING THE BENEFIT PROMISE

Social Security is funded through contributions (taxes) paid by current workers and their employers. Social Security taxes are withheld from employees' paychecks. An employer contribution of the same amount is routed to the Social Security Administration (SSA). Those funds are then disbursed to qualifying Social Security recipients. The payments come entirely from employee taxes and matching employer contributions.

Long-term planners realized capital markets could be used to pay for a large portion of Social Security benefits. If $100 is needed in 30 years, then one need only contribute $23 today, earn 5% per year thereafter and the $100 will be available. This means 23% would be funded by employee taxes and employer contributions and 77% funded by capital markets...and so advance funding was born.

FORECASTING FUTURE EVENTS

Auditors reconcile the past while actuaries make assumptions about the future. No one knows when a person might die, become disabled, retire, or even how much money they will make. Actuaries specialize in modeling future operational needs of a pension plan. They build the model for funding the plan. Actuaries take into account the myriad things that could happen to a member.

The defined benefit plan is established through a trust. This trust is intended to invest its assets to pay for a large portion of the benefit promise (remember the 77%!). By investing and carefully managing the plan contributions, the need for outside sources of plan funding (such as additional government dollars or other taxpayer contributions) is minimized or eliminated. This allows tax revenues to be applied to other government-provided services.

USING TAXPAYER DOLLARS WISELY

Defined benefit plans are an efficient way to use taxpayer dollars (the government employer's share of defined benefit plan contributions) to provide a promised retirement benefit amount. Using a defined benefit plan to provide retirement income often takes less in contributions than needed for other forms of retirement plans. This is due primarily to professional management of the investments in the trust. Investment professionals work to obtain the highest possible rate of returns for an acceptable level of risk (asset volatility) while maintaining low expenses. When compared to passively-managed mutual funds, professionally-managed funds are able to take advantage of active management and alternative investments. Due to the size of most plans, lower fees may be negotiated.

RISKS IN A DEFINED BENEFIT PLAN

Defined benefit plans are not without risk. As has occurred in recent years, plans using capital markets for funding are subject to the risk inherent in these markets. The effects of the 2008 credit crisis caused actuarially-required contributions to increase sharply. This caused officials to re-examine promised benefits. Elected officials and plan trustees evaluated whether the benefit promise and the associated risk continued to be appropriate for their workforce.

LOOKING AHEAD

Public pension fund management is constantly evolving. Management takes place in a competitive environment, and plan sponsors are continually looking for ways to provide competitive retirement benefits for their workforces. Elected officials and other leaders want to meet their communities' needs while managing limited financial resources.

This book is intended to help defined benefit plan trustees understand the risks and decisions they must make for their plans' members. These decisions will both protect the benefits of the members and uphold the role of the trustees. We wrote this book with the intention of providing actionable information to aid you in your role as trustee. We strongly encourage you to seek further training, examination, and study before you embark on a path that may affect your workforce.

2

Purpose of the Actuarial Valuation

ESTIMATING ALL BENEFIT CHECKS THAT WILL EVER BE SENT

Valuation is a simple and well-defined process. The actuary's job is to predict all the benefits that can ever be paid. Then, using a predictive model based on actuarial assumptions, the actuary calculates the value of those benefits in today's dollars. This model has three components, as explained in the next three paragraphs.

Members whose benefits are already being paid are referred to as pay-status members. Their liability to the pension plan is the value in today's dollars of all future retirement checks they (and any beneficiary) are expected to receive. The valuation model estimates how long (the life expectancy) the retiree (and any beneficiary) will remain in pay-status.

For members who are actively working, these future benefit payments will include disability, retirement, termination, and death benefits. The valuation model assesses the likelihood these benefits will ultimately be paid for each active member. These future benefits are then discounted to today's dollars.

Finally, the valuation will combine the liabilities for all groups. The result is the total liabilities of the plan.

INVESTMENT RETURNS ALSO PAY FOR BENEFITS

Benefit payments are funded by two sources of funds: pension plan contributions and returns on investments. The capital markets are expected to make a significant contribution to the payment of benefits, lessening the drain on the plan sponsor's current resources.

But how much will the capital markets contribute toward the funding of these benefits? That depends on the underlying investments and the earnings on those underlying investments. The estimated long-term rate of return is often set by the plan's board of trustees. Actuaries are bound by actuarial standards of practice in their choice of assumptions. Consequently, it is best if the plan's board and actuary can agree on the assumption to be used. This assumption is the expected rate of return the investments generate to fund projected and current benefits.

DISCOUNT RATE VERSUS RATE OF RETURN

It's easiest to think of the difference between the discount rate and the investment rate of return as a difference in direction. Although these two terms are often used interchangeably, the discount rate is most often used when going back in time. When liabilities are calculated in today's dollars, the discount rate is used to bring the value of the future retirement check to today. The future benefit checks are discounted back to today at the assumed rate of return to determine their present value. The rate of return is used for moving forward in time. Today's assets are projected forward at the assumed rate of return to estimate the future market value of assets.

As an example, a volunteer retirement plan's board of directors established the discount rate to use in estimating future plan benefits at 5.5%. This means all future benefit payments were discounted back in time to the valuation date at 5.5%. For the upcoming year, the portfolio is anticipated to earn 6.5%. In this case, an investment return of 6.5%, when the discount rate is 5.5%, creates a positive asset gain to the plan. The investment return of 6.5% exceeds the discount rate of 5.5%.

VALUE THE FUTURE BENEFIT PAYMENTS

The valuation process will tell you the discounted value of all those future benefit payments. In discounting the future benefit payments, the actuary also applies the probabilities of the member terminating employment, retiring, dying, and so forth. This discounted number is known as the **Present Value of Future Benefits**. This number represents an amount that could be placed in the fund today to fund all future benefits (if all assumptions are exactly realized). In other words, the final payment would be paid to the last beneficiary just before he or she dies.

PAYING OFF THE LIABILITY

The present value of future benefits need not be contributed immediately, but how much of the liability should be contributed? *(Recall the previous example where $23 invested over time grows to $100.)*

The actuary will employ a Funding Method to determine the annual contribution.

FUNDING METHOD

A variety of methods exist for determining the annual contribution. These methods are employed to ensure all liabilities are valued. The expectation is when a member retires the future benefits are fully funded. Funding methods develop the normal (annual) cost for the member's benefit. The methods differ in how this normal cost is developed. One funding method may produce a normal cost that remains level as a percent of pay. Another may develop a normal cost that mirrors the value of the benefit accrual in the year. Two common funding methods are the Entry Age Normal Cost method and the Projected Unit Credit method. Most plans in the public sector use the Entry Age Normal method since it produces the most stable costs year over year.

VALUATION PURPOSE: ANNUAL REQUIRED CONTRIBUTION

Two main components comprise the pension plan contribution: the normal cost and the payment on the unfunded accrued liability (UAL). These two actuarial terms will be defined in subsequent paragraphs. Contributions to the plan are deemed to first go to the normal cost, then toward the payment on the unfunded accrued liability.

Priority 1: Keep up on current costs; do not add to the UAL through missed payments

> The **normal cost** is the cost of current year benefit accrual. All funding methods will require a payment on the current period costs. Each funding method will have a different way of defining the current period cost.

Priority 2: Make a payment on amounts in arrears

> The **UAL payment** is an annual payment amount based on the portion of the total present value of benefits allocated for the members' past service. A UAL exists when there are not enough assets in the trust to cover the value of these past service benefits. Different methods exist for developing the payment for the UAL. All funding methods require a payment on this amount.

The annual required contribution is the sum of the Normal Cost and the UAL payment.

THE FUNDAMENTAL EQUATION OF BALANCE

All benefits must be valued; nothing can be omitted.

The sum of future contributions and past contributions **must** equal the present value of all benefits and expenses.

The present value of all benefits **must** equal the present value of the future normal costs plus the accrued liability.

The important and useful point here is the accrued liability can reasonably be thought of as the desired level of assets. In other words, the assets the plan should have had, had all assumptions and contributions been met.

PART II

THE ACTUARIALLY DETERMINED CONTRIBUTION

3

Actuarial Assumptions

THE ACTUARIALLY DETERMINED CONTRIBUTION

The development of the Actuarially Determined Contribution (ADC, pronounced "A-DECK") involves a number of steps:

1. The actuary sets assumptions regarding the future experience of the investments and the members.
2. The actuary requests data from the plan with each valuation.
3. The actuary reviews the data to ensure its continuing reasonableness for use in the valuation process.
4. The actuary uses the asset information to determine the "actuarial value of assets."

During the valuation, each member will have a normal cost and an accrued liability computed on their behalf. Both the normal cost and the accrued liability for the plan are the total of these individual calculations. The UAL is the difference between the assets and the accrued liability. Based on the funding policy of the plan and the assumptions used, the actuary determines the annual required payment to pay down the UAL.

Finally, the actuary adds the normal cost and the payment on the unfunded accrued liability. This total is the ADC.

SETTING THE ACTUARIAL ASSUMPTIONS

Actuaries must use assumptions to model possible future states. Benefits expected to be paid in the future are funded now. The tools used to assess the future are the actuarial assumptions. Two broad categories of actuarial assumptions are used: "economic" assumptions and "demographic" assumptions.

Economic assumptions look at the global assumptions of inflation, real rates of return, payroll growth, and individual salary increases. At their core, these assumptions are all related to inflation.

Demographic assumptions are predictions about what happens to people. These assumptions include death, retirement, termination, or disability.

INFLATION: THE "CORNERSTONE" OF ECONOMIC ASSUMPTIONS

The inflation assumption is the cornerstone of the economic assumptions. At the base of the long-term investment return assumption is inflation. Inflation plus a real rate of return is equal to the nominal, or total, expected rate of return. Payroll growth is the amount the aggregate payroll increases each year and is comprised of inflation plus, possibly, a "productivity" factor. Finally, the annual salary increase assumption is built from inflation, plus productivity, plus a "merit and promotion" assumption. Figure A provides a simple chart showing the nominal rate of return.

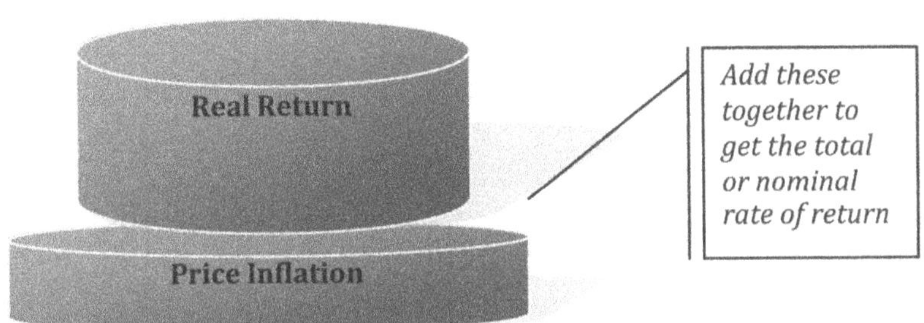

Figure A: Nominal Rate of Return

The valuation process looks at a participant's lifespan from hiring to death. This span can last up to 80 years. Thus, when actuaries talk about the inflation assumption they are speaking of a long period of time. Investment consultants, as will be discussed later, use a much shorter time period. Their time period is typically a five- to 10-year period for the inflation assumption. Knowing the time horizon in any assumption is critical. The time horizon creates differences in the inflation assumption as well as the application of this assumption.

Actuarial funding implies investment returns will pay for a portion of everyone's retirement benefit. In order to estimate the contribution needed today, the actuary estimates to what extent investment returns can be expected to fund the future benefit. The first step is to estimate inflation.

A thorough review of the inflation assumption includes the following:

1. The history of inflation.
2. What your own investment consultant predicts (and for what time horizon).
3. What other investment consultants predict.
4. The rate "implied" in the bond market.

5. The inflation rate assumed by Social Security.
6. The Federal Reserve policy for the rate of inflation.

THE FOLLOWING IS AN EXTRACT FROM AN ECONOMIC ASSUMPTION ANALYSIS FOR A LARGE CITY.

INFLATION ASSUMPTION: LARGE CITY EXAMPLE

"Inflation" refers to price inflation, as measured by annual increases in the Consumer Price Index (CPI). The CPI is calculated by the U.S. Department of Labor's Bureau of Labor Statistics. This inflation assumption underlies other economic assumptions. It impacts investment return, salary increases, and payroll growth. The annual long-term inflation assumption as of 2017 is 2.75%.

HISTORY OF THE CONSUMER PRICE INDEX (CPI-U)

Figure B shows the average annual inflation in each of the 10 consecutive five-year periods over the last 50 years.

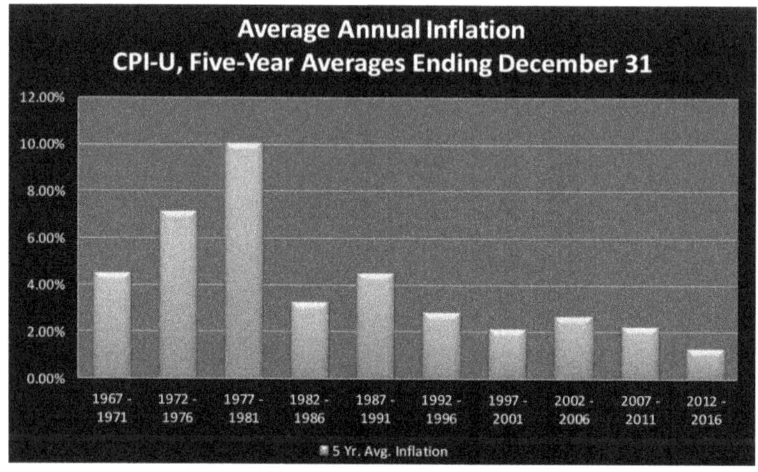

Figure B: Average Annual Inflation CPI-U

Table 2 shows the average inflation over various periods, ending December 31, 2016.

Table 2: Average Annual Inflation over Extended Periods

Average Annual Inflation over longer periods	
Periods Ending December 31, 2016	Average Annual Increase in CPI-U
Last five (5) years	1.36%
Last ten (10) years	1.81%
Last fifteen (15) years	2.10%
Last twenty (20) years	2.12%
Last twenty-five (25) years	2.27%
Last thirty (30) years	2.64%

Source: Bureau of Labor Statistics, CPI-U, all items, not seasonally adjusted

FORECASTS FROM INVESTMENT CONSULTING FIRMS: LARGE CITY EXAMPLE

Most investment consulting firms assume inflation will be less than 2.75%. In 2016, Horizon Actuarial Services, LLC surveyed 12 investment consulting firms about their 20-year or longer inflation rates. The expected rate of inflation for the next 20 years, as measured by the Consumer Price Index of all Urban Consumers (CPI-U), ranged from 2.0% to 2.8%. The median inflation expectation is 2.3%. Their current retained investment consultant assumes inflation will increase at the rate of 2.00% per year over the next 10 years.

EXPECTATIONS IMPLIED IN THE BOND MARKET: LARGE CITY EXAMPLE

Another source of information about future inflation is the market for U.S. Treasury bonds. For example, on December 30, 2016:

- The yield for 20-year inflation-indexed Treasury bonds was 0.82%
- The yield for 20-year non-inflation indexed Treasury bonds was 2.79%

Thus, the bond market was predicting inflation over the next 20 years would average 1.97% (non-indexed of 2.79% less indexed of 0.82%).

The difference in yield between the non-indexed and indexed for 30-year bonds implies 2.05% inflation over the next 30 years. This is consistent with the slow-growth forecasts of inflation and the economy for the next decade. Figure C shows the historical market implied inflation from January 1, 2003 through December 31, 2016.

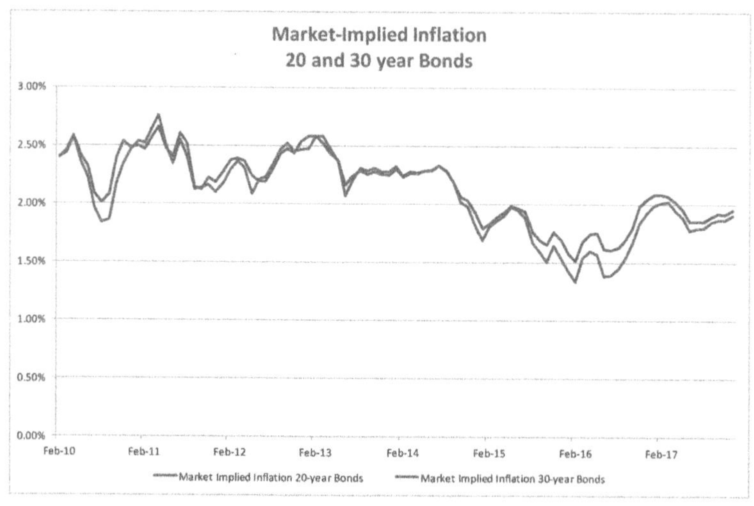

Figure C: Market-Implied Inflation

However, this analysis is known to be imperfect. It ignores the compensation for inflation risk premium buyers of U.S. Treasury bonds often demand. Possible differences in liquidity between U.S. Treasury bonds and Treasury Inflation Protected Securities (TIPS) are also ignored.

FORECASTS FROM SOCIAL SECURITY ADMINISTRATION: LARGE CITY EXAMPLE

Each year the SSA's Office of the Chief Actuary projects a long-term average annual inflation rate. The SSA presents results under three different sets of assumptions: low cost, best estimate, and high cost. The 2016 rate is 2.6% under the best estimate cost assumption.

For the second year in a row, the SSA's Chief Actuary reduced this assumption by 0.10% from the prior year. In addition, the Chief Actuary also narrowed the low cost and high cost scenarios to 2.0% and 3.2% respectively. The Consumer Price Index of Urban Wage Earners and Clerical Workers (CPI-W) has been computed since 1913. This index represents approximately 28% of the population. Table 3 shows the results of these changes.

Table 3: Long-Term Average Annual Inflation Rate

Social Security Trustees' Report CPI-W for the Long-Range (75 year) projection Period					
Trustees Report Alternative 2015			Trustees Report Alternative 2016		
I	II	III	I	II	III
(Low Cost)	(Best Estimate)	(High Cost)	(Low Cost)	Best Estimate	(High Cost)
3.40%	2.70%	2.00%	3.20%	2.60%	2.00%

SURVEY OF PROFESSIONAL FORECASTERS AND FED POLICY: LARGE CITY EXAMPLE

The Philadelphia Federal Reserve conducts a quarterly survey of the Society of Professional Forecasters. Their most recent forecast (fourth quarter 2016) was for inflation to average 2.15% over the 10-year period (2016 through 2025). Most observers expect inflation to continue to be low for the next 10 years.

The Federal Open Market committee (FOMC) targets a 2% Personal Consumption Expenditure (PCE) price index. Since 1992, the PCE has averaged 1.8% while the CPI-U averaged 2.3%. The last 70 years saw a PCE of 3.1% and a CPI-U of 3.5%. This index includes all professionals, self-employed individuals, retirees, clerical workers, and others receiving regular income. To estimate long term inflation, this method takes the sum of the targeted PCE and the average difference between CPI-U and the PCE.

FOMC Target for price increases	2.00%
Average difference between CPI-U and the PCE	0.50%
Inflation assumption (2% plus .5%)	2.50%

In this example, 2.50% was the recommended long-term inflation assumption.

INVESTMENT RETURN ASSUMPTION: LARGE CITY EXAMPLE

The investment return assumption is a key assumption used in any actuarial valuation of a retirement plan. It is used to discount future expected benefit payments to the valuation date in order to determine the liabilities of the plan. Even a small change to this assumption can produce significant changes to liabilities and contribution rates. Currently, this large city example plan assumes future investment returns will average 7.75% per year. This example plan also assumes that the investment return will earn enough to cover their administrative expenses. That implies the assumed investment return is 7.75% plus the administrative expenses.

The nominal or total assumed rate of return in this example is 7.75%. The inflation assumption in this case is 2.75% per year. The real rate of return is defined as the difference between the nominal rate of return and the inflation rate. In this example, the real rate of return is 5.00%.

Nominal rate of return	7.75%
Inflation rate	2.75%
Real rate of return (Nominal less inflation)	5.00%

Since the inflation assumption has already been discussed, much of the analysis that follows focuses on the real rate of return assumption of 5.00% per year.

Figure D is a chart showing a history of market returns for this example through fiscal year (FY) 2016.

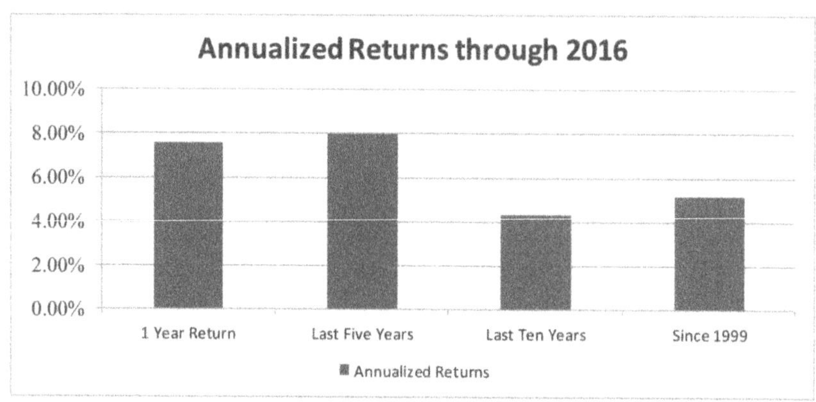

Figure D: Annualized Returns

Past performance is not a reliable indicator of future performance for this assumption. The actual asset allocation of the trust fund impacted the overall performance of the trust. The real rates of return for many asset classes, especially equities, vary dramatically from year to year. Even a 20-year period is not long enough to provide reasonable guidance. For this reason, the next step in the process in the analysis is to determine an estimate of the expected real rate of return. This analysis focuses on the future expectations of the asset classes as applied to the target asset allocation.

Your target asset allocation is unique to your fund. Your target sets out guidelines for the proportion of your invested assets you will have in each asset class. You may have a target asset allocation of 50% in equities and 50% in fixed income, or you may have a target asset allocation that includes many additional asset categories. These categories include private equity, hedge funds, international equity, international fixed, and alternatives.

Many of your public sector peer group board members undertake this exercise of setting long-term investment return assumptions. The Figure E is a chart showing the distribution of the investment return assumptions in the Public Plans Data for 2016-2017 valuations of 96 public sector retirement plans.

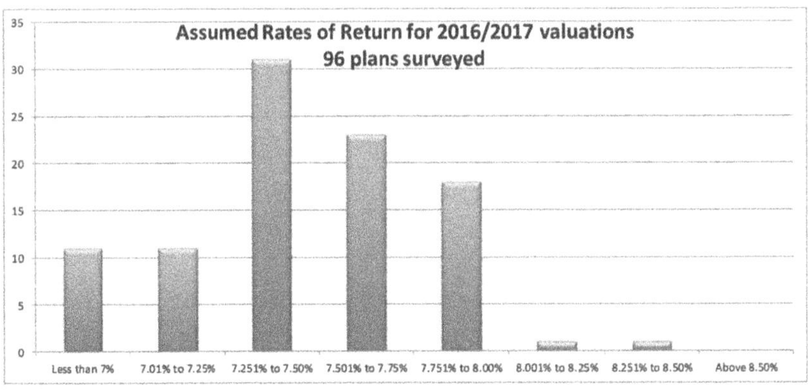

Figure E: Assumed Rates of Return 2016-2017

Source: Public Plans Database (n=96)

EXPENSES NETTED OUT OF RETURN: LARGE CITY EXAMPLE

For this example, the current return assumption is 7.75%, after subtracting all investment and administrative expenses. This assumption implies the trust must earn 7.75% plus the expenses (since the trust pays those expenses by subtracting them from the investment returns). A plan's expenses must be estimated when recommending the investment return assumption.

Table 4 shows the administrative expenses for a recent six-year period. These expenses are expressed as a percentage of the assets, adjusted for cash flow, each year.

Table 4: Administrative Expenses 2011-2016 (inclusive)

Fiscal Year	Administrative Expense
2016	0.19%
2015	0.19%
2014	0.18%
2013	0.19%
2012	0.19%
2011	0.17%
Average	**0.18%**

When expenses are paid out of returns you will need to earn the assumed rate of 7.75% PLUS the .18%

Using the information in Table 4, 0.18% (18 basis points) of each year's investment return is assumed to be used to pay administrative expenses. This assumption is then used in setting the investment return assumption.

ASSET ALLOCATION: LARGE CITY EXAMPLE

The most appropriate approach to selecting an investment return assumption is to identify expected returns. Factors considered include a fund's asset allocation mapped to forward-looking capital market assumptions. No longer do pension plans just rely on stocks and bonds as the investment vehicles for the plans. Table 5 provides a summary of the asset allocation used in our analysis.

Table 5: Asset Allocation for Large City Example

Asset Class	Allocation (Percent of Total Portfolio)
Domestic Equity	22.50%
International Equity	23.50%
Domestic Fixed Income	15.50%
International Fixed Income	2.50%
Real Estate	8.00%
Private Equity/Hedge Fund/Alternatives	20.00%
Other	8.00%
Total	**100.00%**

Your asset allocation will have each consultant's asset class expectations applied

CAPITAL MARKET EXPECTATION: LARGE CITY EXAMPLE

Capital markets are markets for buying and selling equity and debt instruments (such as stocks and bonds). Investment consulting firms periodically issue reports describing their capital market assumptions. Investments are divided into two categories. These categories are "core investments" and "alternative investments." The estimates for core investments are generally based on anticipated returns produced by passive index funds after investment-related fees are subtracted. The investment return expectations for the alternative investments are also net of investment expenses.

Since investment expenses are included in the expected return estimates, no further adjustment to the analysis for investment expenses is needed. Administrative expenses are not included in the expected return estimates. Costs to administer a retirement plan will vary widely by plan. Administrative expenses are only estimates. They are either paid for through returns in excess of the actuarial assumed rate or added directly to the annual contribution requirement for the plan. Administrative expenses may also be paid by the entity contributing to the plan (usually the employer).

There two types of management strategies: active and passive. Some investment funds use active management investment strategies. Active management is the use of people, such as a single manager, co-managers, or a team of managers to manage a fund's portfolio. Active managers rely on analytical research, forecasts, and their own judgment and experience in making investment decisions as to which securities to buy, hold, and sell. These strategies have higher investment expenses compared to strategies investing in passive index funds. Passively-managed index funds mirror the components of a stock market index. For example, the well-known Vanguard 500 fund mirrors the daily activity of the Standard & Poor's 500 Index.

The model just discussed only uses indexed fund expected returns, as shown in Table 6. Alpha, or the extra return presumed from active management, is generally not permitted to be used in setting the investment return assumption. The actuarial standards of practice permit an exception when sufficient justification is presented. Table 6 depicts Capital Market Assumptions for this example.

Table 6: Capital Market Assumptions

Capital Market Assumptions-Large City Example- as of December 31, 2015			
10-Year Horizon	Expected Return	Asset Mix	Arithmetic Return
Asset Class	From Consultant	Trust Allocation	Product (Expected Return times Trust Allocation)
U.S. Equity	7.69%	22.50%	1.73%
International Equity	8.12%	23.50%	1.91%
Core Fixed Income	3.61%	18.00%	0.65%
High Yield	6.77%	0.00%	0.00%
Emerging Markets Debt	6.24%	0.00%	0.00%
Global REITS	6.23%	2.78%	0.17%
Commodities	4.50%	21.00%	0.95%
Private Markets	12.40%	7.00%	0.87%
Private Real Estate	6.62%	5.22%	0.35%
Summary		100.00%	6.62%

For the survey analysis the following firms were used:

- BNY Mellon
- Hewitt EnnisKnupp
- JP Morgan
- New England Pension Consultants (NEPC)
- Mercer Consulting
- Pension Consulting Alliance (PCA)
- RV Kuhns
- Wilshire

From each firm we receive the expected returns by asset class and the correlations between the various asset classes. The correlation is a measurement of how one asset class moves in relation to another. The correlation between asset classes is used to assess the impact of volatility on the portfolio. Table 7 provides the Arithmetic Return for this example.

Table 7: Arithmetic Return (No Volatility Considered): Large City Example

Investment Consultant (1)	Consultant Expected Nominal Return for your (2)	Investment Consultant Inflation Assumption (3)	Real Return (2)-(3) for your Portfolio (4)	Actuary's Inflation Assumption for your Portfolio (5)	Nominal Return (4)+(5) for your Portfolio (6)	Investment Expenses for your Portfolio (7)	Nominal Return Net of Expenses for your Portfolio (6)-(7) (8)
1	7.01%	2.50%	4.51%	2.50%	7.01%	0.18%	6.83%
2	6.76%	2.20%	4.56%	2.50%	7.06%	0.18%	6.88%
3	6.62%	1.56%	5.06%	2.50%	7.56%	0.18%	7.38%
4	7.45%	2.26%	5.19%	2.50%	7.69%	0.18%	7.51%
5	7.48%	2.25%	5.23%	2.50%	7.73%	0.18%	7.55%
6	7.26%	2.00%	5.26%	2.50%	7.76%	0.18%	7.58%
7	7.86%	2.25%	5.61%	2.50%	8.11%	0.18%	7.93%
8	8.26%	2.20%	6.06%	2.50%	8.56%	0.18%	8.38%
Average	**7.34%**	**2.15%**	**5.18%**	**2.50%**	**7.68%**	**0.18%**	**7.50%**

Expected return is 7.50% without volatility, so it is on the HIGH side of expected returns.

Table 7 illustrates, based on averages from the firms we surveyed, the expected return for one year would be 7.50% for a typical portfolio. This expected return is based on an inflation assumption of 2.50%, an expected real return of 5.18%, and expected expenses of 0.18%.

The preceding model does not account for portfolio volatility. Volatility may reduce returns. The next analysis looks at the expectations, given the assumed levels of volatility for this particular asset allocation.

GEOMETRIC RETURN (WITH VOLATILITY CONSIDERED)

The plan's nominal rate of return includes two components. The two components are the plan's current asset allocation and its investment consultant's capital market assumption. The average compound nominal return, after subtracting investment and administrative expenses, is provided in Table 8. This provides the 40th, 50th, and 60th percentiles (percentile indicates a certain percentage falls below that percentile) of the 10-year geometric average of the expected nominal return, after subtracting expenses.

Table 8: Expected Annual Geometric Returns and Return Probabilities

Expected Annual Geometric Returns and Return Probabilities					
Investment Consultant	Distribution of 10-Year Average Geometric Net Nominal Return			Probability of exceeding	
	40th	50th	60th	7.75%	7.50%
1	5.07%	6.08%	7.09%	33.83%	36.12%
2	5.42%	6.31%	7.19%	34.06%	36.69%
3	5.79%	6.73%	7.67%	39.21%	41.80%
4	6.06%	6.94%	7.83%	40.84%	43.62%
5	5.85%	6.83%	7.83%	40.76%	43.24%
6	5.98%	6.92%	7.87%	41.26%	43.87%
7	5.88%	7.00%	8.14%	43.37%	45.58%
8	6.69%	7.67%	8.66%	49.19%	51.75%
Average	**5.84%**	**6.81%**	**7.79%**	**40.31%**	**42.83%**

In the preceding table, a 40% probability exists that the funds will earn less than 5.84%. A 50% probability exists that the funds will earn less than 6.81%, and there is a 60% probability of earning less than 7.79%. This implies a 40 % probability of earning 7.79% or more.

The investment consultant's capital market assumptions are based on a 10-year investment horizon in the preceding analysis. Most pension investment management teams use 10 years for developing and monitoring their investment strategies. While this seems short in terms of the length of time the pension fund will exist, it is important to recall in most plans, due to the increasing retirements of the baby boom generation, a large portion of liabilities will be paid out in the next 10 years. A pension fund cannot earn returns on money it has already paid out.

The investment return assumption used in the actuarial valuation has a much longer investment horizon.

Volatility in an investment portfolio costs money. Volatility may decrease returns. Think of a fund over a four-year period. The fund earns 7% each year. The arithmetic return (add the returns and divide by four) is 7% and the geometric return is also 7%. But now think of that same fund earning 0%, 14%, 0%, and 14%. The arithmetic return is also 7%. However, the compounded return is 6.77%. The volatility cost in this example is the difference between the two geometric returns, or 0.23%.

As shown in Table 8, when volatility is considered, the expectation is 50% of the time the retirement funds in the trust will achieve 6.81%. This difference between 7.50% and 6.81% is the cost of volatility. (This is also referred to as the difference between the arithmetic return and the geometric return).

In recommending an assumption rate, the actuary usually looks at both the arithmetic return (the "high" side) and the geometric return (the "low" side). The recommendation for the assumption may fall in between these two calculations. It is also possible that a margin for adverse deviation in experience is desired; then the assumption might even fall below the arithmetic return.

Think of expected investment returns as the sum of a risk-free rate of return and a risk premium. This is the fundamental premise in the Capital Asset Pricing Model (CAPM) used in Modern Portfolio Theory. Riskier investments carry a higher risk premium to compensate the investor for increased uncertainty. Generally, the risk premium for each asset class is constant over long periods of time. Differences may occur in the risk-free return, depending on the investor's time horizon. A risk-free investment has a certain expected return. The risk-free investment has no default or reinvestment risk. Based on this definition, a reasonable benchmark for the risk-free rate is a zero coupon U.S. Treasury security. Thus a 10-year risk-free rate is set equal to the current yield of a 10-year zero coupon U.S. Treasury bond.

SALARY INCREASE RATES- IN GENERAL

The "salary scale" is the component of the actuarial assumptions relating to a member's pay increases over time.

Generally, the salary scale assumption consists of a wage inflation assumption for all members. For members early in their careers, a "merit and promotion increase" is also assumed. Historically, wage inflation almost always exceeds price inflation. This implies employers pay "more than inflation" in order to retain their workforce. Wage inflation is the result of (1) price inflation, and (2) productivity gains being passed through to wages. Since 1951, wage inflation has been about 1.00% a year greater than price inflation but has been trending down in recent years. Figure F depicts the components of salary increases, including the wage inflation components.

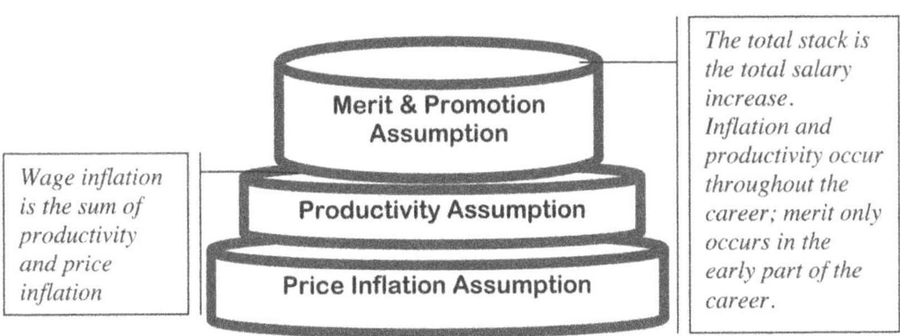

Figure F: Wage Inflation and Salary Increases

Salary increases for governmental employees can vary significantly from year to year. This is common, especially where the recognized bargaining unit is a union. Experience across many governmental plans shows this trend. In many actuarial valuations, the trend of salary increases is to be low for several years followed by a significant increase due to negotiated contracts.

As an example, a union and a fire district negotiate a three-year contract. The union members receive a 1% raise on the first day of the new year and a 0.5% increase on September 1 of the same year. The second year the union members receive 0.5% on the first day of the 2nd calendar year. Union members receive 3.25% January 1 in the third year.

Therefore, particular data over a longer period will be reviewed when establishing the assumptions. For this analysis, we reviewed a 10-year period but ultimately our conclusions were based on the five-year analysis.

WAGE INFLATION (PRICE INFLATION PLUS PRODUCTIVITY ASSUMPTIONS) AND SALARY INCREASES - IN GENERAL

Salary increases are comprised of three pieces: price inflation, productivity, and merit. Inflation is the price inflation discussed previously. Productivity is the amount above inflation all members are assumed to receive in their annual pay increases.

Finally, merit is the portion of the increase for the newer employees. Promotions, new skills, and additional educational degrees are included in this component.

Salary increases for longer-service employees are almost entirely wage inflation. These employees receive most of their promotions and merit increases early in their career. Their acquisition of advanced degrees or skills has already occurred. Many of the factors resulting in pay increases are largely inapplicable or have diminished importance for longer-service employees.

MERIT AND PROMOTION ASSUMPTIONS - IN GENERAL

Salary increases for shorter-service employees typically include wage inflation and a component for merit and promotion. A sample schedule of merit increases during the first seven years of employment is shown in Table 9. Data observed in the study indicate merit increases were generally in line with the current assumptions.

Table 9: Analysis of Merit Increases

Service Based Salary Scale Analysis of Merit Increases		
Years of Service	Actual Merit Increase	Expected Merit Increase
1	6.46%	5.25%
2	6.33%	5.00%
3	5.32%	4.00%
4	4.04%	3.00%
5	1.77%	2.00%
6	1.15%	1.00%
7	0.72%	0.50%
>7	0.52%	0.00%

Active members with one year of service received an average merit increase of 6.46% compared to the current assumption of 5.25%. Merit increases for members with seven years of service were 0.72% compared to the assumption of 0.50%. The increases for members with one to four years of service are slightly higher than the current assumption. The 10-year data showed slightly smaller differences. The actual increases for members with five to seven years of service were generally in line with the current assumptions. Table 10 shows the total assumed salary scale over the preceding seven years.

Table 10: Assumed Total Salary Scale

Assumed Total Salary Scale Including Price Inflation, Productivity and Merit				
Years of Service	Price Inflation (a)	Productivity (b)	Merit and Promotion (c)	Total Annual Increase (a)+(b)+(c)
1	2.50%	0.50%	5.25%	8.25%
2	2.50%	0.50%	5.00%	8.00%
3	2.50%	0.50%	4.00%	7.00%
4	2.50%	0.50%	3.00%	6.00%
5	2.50%	0.50%	2.00%	5.00%
6	2.50%	0.50%	1.00%	4.00%
7	2.50%	0.50%	0.50%	3.50%
>7	2.50%	0.50%	0.00%	3.00%

This assumption could also be by age, or by a combination of age and service.

PAYROLL GROWTH RATE

The rate of salary increases just discussed are assumptions applied to an individual member's annual raise. These salary amounts are used to project the individual member's future benefits. Contributions to the plan are expressed as a percent of pay. The total payroll amount is used to estimate the amount of contributions to the trust for the year.

When determining the annual amount to fund the UAL, a payroll growth assumption may be used. This assumption reflects total payroll increases every year, resulting in an increase in expected contributions. Since the contribution amount is a percent of payroll, when payroll increases the contribution dollar amount increases.

As payroll increases over time, contribution amounts also increase. The assumed growth in payroll is frequently equal to the wage inflation assumption. In the preceding case, the payroll growth assumption is equal to the sum of the price inflation assumption and the productivity assumption. This amount is 2.50% plus 0.50%, or a 3.00% payroll growth assumption.

When the payroll growth assumption is "high," the initial payment on the UAL is lower. The earlier payments are lower because payments are assumed to grow in the future. A "low" payroll growth assumption leads to contributing higher amounts in the earlier years to fund the UAL. A "zero" payroll growth assumption leads to a level dollar amount for the annual payment of the UAL.

Payroll may grow at a rate different from the average pay increase for individual members. Three reasons contribute to this variation. First, when older, longer-service members leave, retire, or die, their replacements are generally new members at a lower salary. Second, in most stable populations the growth in total payroll will generally be smaller than the average pay increase for members. Finally, payroll also grows due to an increase in the size of the group.

In developing a funding policy, there is frequently an objective to have the cost for the pension stay in sync with payroll costs. For that reason, many plans may adopt a funding policy that recognizes pension costs will grow at the same rate as payroll.

Figure G is a chart showing the impact of the payroll growth assumption on the growth in the amortization payments. The assumed "no growth" in payroll shows the same flat dollar amount of amortization payment every year. This "no growth" scenario is also referred to as a "level dollar" amortization method. The larger payroll growth assumption leads to the lower initial payment. The larger payroll growth assumption also leads to the steeper increase in the dollar amount of the annual payment.

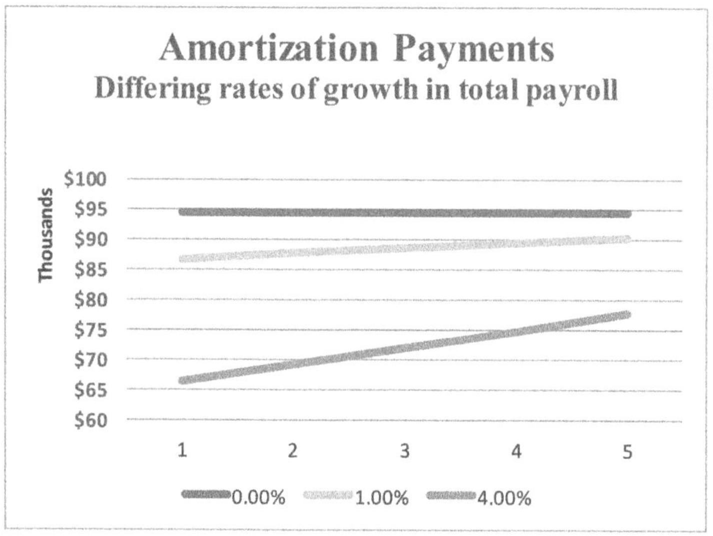

Figure G: Amortization Payments

4

Participant Data

POST-RETIREMENT MORTALITY RATES

How long will checks need to be sent to the retiree? This is determined by how long the retiree (or retiree and beneficiary) will live.

When choosing an appropriate mortality assumption, actuaries typically use standard mortality tables. These tables can be adjusted to reflect various characteristics of the covered group, and to provide for expectations of future mortality improvement (both up to and after the measurement date). If the plan population has sufficient credibility (meaning it is large enough) to justify its own mortality table, then the use of such a table could also be appropriate. Factors that may be considered in selecting and/or adjusting a mortality table include the demographics of the covered group, the size of the group, the statistical credibility of the group's experience, and future mortality improvement.

Setting assumptions for life expectancy has two parts. First, there is a probability of death that is determined at each age. These probabilities are laid out in a table by age. The mortality table currently being recommended is a standard table published by the Society of Actuaries (SOA) called the RP-2014 Mortality table. There is also a projection scale that is used to project future improvements in mortality for future generations. The most current projection scale is the MP 2017 (short for "mortality projection 2017").

Combining the mortality table with the MP 2017 scale creates a set of mortality rates that "improve" with each generation. This type of table (or series of tables) is called generational mortality. Future mortality rates will be projected to continually decrease each year in the future. A decrease in the mortality rate increases life expectancy. Therefore, the life expectancy at age 60 for someone reaching 60 now will not be as long as the life expectancy for someone reaching 60 in 2020, and this person's life expectancy will not be as long as someone reaching 60 in 2040, and so forth. The table has separate rates for males and females.

In Table 11, 59 male retirees died during the last five years. The current assumptions predicted 82 (81.6) deaths would occur. Since there are fewer deaths, the members are living longer than assumed. The "actual deaths to expected deaths (A/E)" ratio is shown in the column labeled "A/E ratio." Actuarial standards recommend assumptions for mortality have margins for future improvements in mortality. Actuaries will generally set mortality rates so the A/E ratio is 100%. The MP 2017 scale is then applied to the table. The MP scale will create the margin for future mortality improvements.

Table 11: Actual Deaths to Expected Deaths

Post-Retirement Mortality (non-disabled) – Males RP-2000 White Collar with Generational Improvements					
	Based on last 5 years			Based on a new table	
Age	Actual deaths	Expected deaths (from mortality table)	A/E ratio	Expected deaths (from new mortality table)	Actual Deaths to Expected Deaths (A/E) ratio
50 - 54	0	0.3	0.00%	0.3	0.00%
55 - 59	2	1.5	133.33%	1.4	142.86%
60 - 64	3	6	50.00%	5.5	54.55%
65 - 69	9	12.1	74.38%	6	150.00%
70 - 74	11	9.8	112.24%	9	122.22%
75 - 79	5	10.6	47.17%	7	71.43%
80 - 84	9	15.6	57.69%	8	112.50%
85 - 89	12	14.1	85.11%	10	120.00%
90 and over	8	11.6	68.97%	11	72.73%
Totals	**59**	**81.6**	**72.30%**	**58.2**	**101.37%**
** Assumed based on the same group of exposures and actual deaths*					

For the mortality assumption, 72.3% would be considered too low. The actuary will recommend moving to a new table where the A/E ratio is closer to 100%. The new table proposed shows an A/E ratio of 101.37%. This is a ratio much more appropriate for the mortality assumption.

Other assumptions such as disability, retirement, and termination are also studied by examining an A/E ratio.

Note on data credibility: The experience of the group needs to be credible for the data to be usable when making a decision. Data are credible when the population is large. Smaller populations exhibit data that are too easily swayed by single events. Long term decisions should not be made based on singular events. The preceding example uses a very small set of data. The example shows how the analysis is conducted and is not meant to be an indication of the credibility of that group.

ROLE OF PARTICIPANT DATA

Valuation is a process whose objective is to produce a reasonable estimate of the benefit payments to be paid. The process is "redone" each year using updated data for active members and updating data for the retirees already receiving benefits.

The valuation is a self-correcting process. Each year the contribution rate is recalibrated to the new data. New retirees are added to the rolls. Member data is updated for changes in pay and service. New members are added to the roster. The liabilities and ADCs are updated to account for the new data.

Each year the participant data (members, retirees, terminated members with deferred benefit) are sent to the actuary. The actuary will "trace" where everyone was at the both the beginning and the end of the year. This trace is commonly referred to as the "status reconciliation matrix." This process ensures members do not "go missing" and that entire groups of members are not overlooked.

The actuary will review the data for reasonableness but will not audit the data. Using some fairly common "business rules," the actuary will prepare a set of questions to confirm the data. The actuary uses analytical skills to question the data for outliers.

Business rules when data should be double-checked include:

- A member's pay increases by more than 20%
- A member's pay decreases
- A member's date of birth changes
- A retiree benefit amount unexpectedly changes
- A new hire is too young
- A new hire enters the plan with past service

Business rules are established by working with data and gaining an understanding of what can reasonably be expected in the data.

The following is an example of a data reconciliation process:

As 2016 began, the city of Paley, Anystate began the year with 100 active employees. This city was established more than 50 years ago. Former employees and their post-death beneficiaries number 500 individuals currently receiving benefits. Twenty-five people previously worked for the city but are not yet receiving benefits. These individuals are not yet retirement age.

During 2016, Paley hired 30 new employees. Twenty individuals left the city with accrued benefits but were not old enough to receive them. The city also celebrated 10 employees' retirements during the year. Five former employees retired during the year. The retirement fund lost 30 individuals to death. Five of the current members will be able to draw their pensions in 2017 while the other 25 former employees are not yet eligible to draw pensions.

The city's plan has the same number of participants at both the beginning and end of the year. The Table 12 shows a status reconciliation matrix of Paley's participants in its retirement fund.

Table 12: Status Reconciliation Matrix

City of Paley, Anystate Retirement Plan Status Reconciliation Matrix				
Status	Actives	Terminated with deferred benefit	Retired (in pay status)	Total
Beginning of year	100	25	500	625
New hires	30			30
Terminated with deferred benefit	-20	20		0
Died		-5	-25	-30
Retired	-10	-5	15	0
End of year	100	35	490	625

The ultimate goal of the valuation process is to predict all the benefits to be paid. Actuarial assumptions are used to value those benefits. The funding method is then used to determine a contribution requirement for the year. With each valuation, the liabilities are recalibrated to the current group of retirees and members. A data-based valuation is most frequently performed every year, although smaller plans may opt to have a data-based valuation performed every other year.

Actuaries spend time with the data checking for reasonableness. They make sure members haven't gone missing or just "show up."

Data validate experience. Looking at the data helps trustees to see the extent to which the assumptions are adequately projecting the benefits to be paid.

5

Asset Valuation

ASSET VALUATION

Policy Perspective: *A core objective found in many funding policies is to "control and manage contribution rate volatility." Smoothing investment returns alleviates the decision-making that could occur on short-term noise and fluctuations in the capital markets.*

Trust assets are valued at the end of the fiscal year. The valuation of each asset is performed on the basis of its market value. From there, the auditors prepare financial statements displaying the assets. Financial statements are composed of several schedules.

The first schedule is the **"balance sheet."** Balance sheets are snapshots of a financial situation as of a certain date—normally the end of the fiscal year. Each asset is scheduled as of a point in time: the end of the fiscal year. One way to think of a balance sheet is as a statement for "what we have" at the end of the year.

The next schedule is the **"income and expense statement."** Income and expense schedules are more like a video, explaining how the trust changed from the beginning of the year to the end of the year. The income and expense statement reconciles the money coming into and out of the plan. Items coming into the plan include contributions, dividends, and investment appreciation. Items leaving the plan include benefit payments, contribution refunds, and investment and administrative expenses.

One of the important points in reviewing these schedules is making sure the ending balance on each schedule is the same and the beginning balance matches the prior schedule's ending balance. This tells us the assets on hand have been derived from the transactions that occurred during the year (and no assets have been dropped or incorrectly scheduled).

Next, the actuary applies the appropriate "asset return smoothing" method to prepare the actuarial value of assets. The asset return smoothing method is adopted into the funding policy of the trust. The most common method is a five-year smoothing of the investment returns. The asset returns each year are spread over a five-year period. Smoothing techniques have been around for a long time and are extremely common in public sector pension funding. These techniques are employed to minimize decision-making (particularly on contribution rates) that could occur on short term "noise" in the capital markets.

This means for many funds there are layers for each year of an asset gain or loss.

For example, assume the current year is 2022. The trust has recently experienced investment returns both above and below the assumed rate of return. Further assume the plan uses a five-year smoothing method and the asset gains and losses (asset gains and losses are amounts above/below the assumed rate of return) are shown in Table 13.

Table 13: Asset Gain/Loss

Valuation/Fiscal Year	*Original gain or (loss)(returns above/below the assumed rate)*	*Annual Phase-in (assuming no interest for simplicity)*	*Amount previously recognized*	*Amount yet to be recognized (after annual phase-in recognition)*
	(a)	(b)=(a/5)	(c)=(b)*years from 2022	(d)=(a)-(b)-(c)
2018 Amount	$100,000	$20,000	$80,000	$0
2019 Amount	-$50,000	-$10,000	-$30,000	-$10,000
2020 Amount	$200,000	$40,000	$80,000	$80,000
2021 Amount	$10,000	$2,000	$2,000	$6,000
2022 Amount	-$5,000	-$1,000	$0	-$4,000
Total	$255,000	$51,000	$132,000	$72,000

All earnings are eventually recognized. For each year the gain or loss is phased in over a five-year period.

Table 13 tells the following about the actuarial value of assets:

(a) Over the last five years the trust had a net gain of $255,000 on a market value basis (this is the gain over the assumed earnings).

(b) For the 2022 valuation $51,000 will be recognized in the actuarial value of assets.

(c) As of the 2022 valuation, $132,000 of the $255,000 has already been recognized.

(d) At the conclusion of the 2022 valuation, $72,000 of gains will be recognized.

Knowing gains from prior years are still to be recognized portends a downward pressure on the contribution rate. This pressure is released over the next five years. This relief on the contribution rate is due to the inflow of these gains into the actuarial value of the assets. Deferred gains in the actuarial value of assets predict a "tilt" upward in the funded ratio. Deferred losses predict a downward tilt in future funded ratios.

The trustees may also want some additional "insurance" that the actuarial value of assets will always stay within a certain boundary around the market value of assets. Plans with this objective will frequently use an asset "corridor." For example, a 20% corridor means the actuarial value of assets, by definition, cannot ever be more than 20% greater or lower than the market value of assets. The most common corridor is 20%, but other corridor amounts may be used.

6

Normal Cost

Each year, an active plan member will accrue an additional year of retirement benefit. For many plans this annual accrual takes the form of an additional year of service. The increase in the accrual is due to the increase in years of service and any increase in pay.

Some plans, most typically a volunteer firefighter plan, may have an additional accrual in the form of a flat dollar amount for the completion of another year of service.

The funding method dictates the precise way the normal (annual) cost is to be calculated. Plan sponsors (or the board of trustees) select a funding policy that fits their intention for funding. Some may choose a policy that strives to keep costs level as a percent of payroll. Others may use a flat dollar amount for their funding policy. The funding policy for plans will focus on requiring the normal cost is paid each year. This is similar to paying off your current bills as they come due.

Further, the intention of the funding method is to ensure the normal cost for each member is paid as they are hired. The normal cost is paid each year as part of the annual contribution. If all assumptions about investments and about the member are met, the amount of assets contributed on behalf of that member will fully fund all future retirement benefits.

As an example, assume the benefit promise is that the member will receive $10 per month per year of service worked. The accruals and accrued benefit are shown in Table 14.

Table 14: Accruals and Accrued Benefit

Annual Accrual	$120	$120	$120	$120	$120	$120	$120	$120
Accrued Benefit	$120	$240	$360	$480	$600	$720	$840	$960
Years to Retirement	25	24	23	22	21	20	19	18

When the member reaches retirement age, $120 per year of service will be paid for a lifetime. The total value at retirement age of that monthly benefit is $1,500. (*This value is estimated and used for illustration only*)

The contribution does not have to be $1,500. That is because the $120 is not due to be paid until the member's actual retirement date. Actuarial funding is the sharing of costs between contributions and investment earnings. The normal cost is therefore $1,500, but it is discounted for the expected investment earnings. Assume the member is 25 years away from retirement. The trust is expected to earn 7% per year. The normal cost would be $276.37. (This assumes the member has no other benefits that could be paid prior to retirement age).

The balance of the $1,500 required at the member's retirement date will be paid for through the investment earnings of the trust. Thus, for this accrual, contributions pay for 18% of the benefit while investment earnings contribute 82% of the benefit.

To recap, the $276.37 is contributed today and grows by 7% each year for the next 25 years. The contribution accumulates to the value of $1,500 at the member's retirement date.

7

Accrued Liability

The accrued liability is often thought of as the "desired amount of assets." The ratio of the accrued liability to the assets characterizes the funded status of the plan. When that ratio is 100% (accrued liability equals the assets) then the plan is said to be fully funded.

The accrued liability could be viewed as the current value of all those past normal costs. If all normal costs had been contributed and all assumptions met, the value of all past normal costs (with their accumulated investment return) would equal the assets.

What does it mean when there is an unfunded amount?

The UAL is the difference between the accrued liability and the assets. The term "unfunded" illustrates the amount that needs to be "made up" to stay on track to pay the difference between the assets and the accrued liability.

The second part of any contribution requirement is the payment toward the UAL. Many different payment methods may be used to pay off the UAL. Ideally, the payment method is part of the written funding policy.

A UAL can develop for a variety of reasons including:

- Actuarial assumptions may not be met. Around 2008 and 2009 the great recession caused significant investment losses. Those returns were less than the assumed rates of return (assumed returns averaged 8%). The losses created an UAL.
- A UAL can emerge if benefits are granted that include past service.

Table 15 shows annual accruals with a modification.

Table 15: Annual Accruals with Modification

Annual Accrual	$120	$120	$120	$120	$120	$120	$120	$120
Accrued Benefit	$120	$240	$360	$480	$600	$720	$840	$960
Years to Retirement	25	24	23	22	21	20	19	18
Amend all benefits to $12 per month								
Annual Accrual	$144	$144	$144	$144	$144	$144	$144	$144
Accrued Benefit	$144	$288	$432	$576	$720	$864	$1,008	$1,152
Years to Retirement	25	24	23	22	21	20	19	18

In Table 15, benefits were amended in the 7th year (18 years until retirement) from $10 per month per year of service to $12 per month per year of service. The accrued benefit was immediately increased from $960 to $1,152. This is a 20% increase.

The normal cost calculated "back then" would not have included the value of the amended benefit. The funding of the past service benefit would not be handled through normal cost (since that component of cost is based only on the accruals in the current year). Rather, the funding for the past service benefit is handled in accordance with the funding policy for UALs. This means the sponsor's contribution increases over time.

8

Unfunded Accrued Liability

PAYING OFF THE UNFUNDED ACCRUED LIABILITY

Policy Perspective: *A UAL is not necessarily bad. The policy for the plan is to include a reasonable and achievable method for paying off the unfunded accrued liability.*

The previous chapter outlined how the UAL is developed. There are three primary pieces in paying down the UAL. Each piece is derived from an underlying funding policy.

These three pieces are:

1. The length of time for payment (e.g. 20 years)
2. The growth in the payment (will it be a level dollar payment each year or is it anticipated to grow as payroll grows? Or is the payment assumed to grow at some other rate?)
3. The payoff of the UAL (open or closed amortization).

An amortization policy determines the length of time and the structure on the increase or decrease in contributions necessary to pay down the UAL or the surplus. Open amortization (or non-decreasing period amortization) is falling out of favor as more plans are working to pay off principal with each UAL payment.

Specific policy objectives to be outlined and incorporated into any funding policy include:

1. Should changes in the UAL be paid off assuming a level dollar amount each year, or a level percent of payroll each year? Or is there another choice?
2. Should the policy treat the sources of the changes in the UAL differently?
    a. Experience gains and losses
    b. Changes in actuarial assumptions and methods
    c. Benefit plan changes
3. What level and duration of negative amortization (where the payments do not touch the principal) should be allowed?
4. How will the funding support additional objectives of transparency and accountability?
    a. The valuation should reflect the history of the sources and treatment of changes in the UAL.
    b. The amortization policy should have a target date for full funding (as an example, this implies that the policy would not support a target of 80% funding).
5. The amortization of surplus (when assets exceed the accrued liability) should have its own policy.
    a. Should some surplus be "held back" altogether?
    b. Upon entering a surplus position should the plan consider "de-risking"?

Most common policies that emerge from these goals include the following:

1. A general preference for level percent of pay amortization

   a. This means the amortization payment is lower than the level dollar method in early years, but it will cross over at some point in time.

2. Multiple, fixed amortization layers
   a. Setting up a new layer each year.
   b. Possible a new layer each year for each source of change in UAL.

3. The ideal amortization period is 15 to 20 years
   a. 15 years gives too little "volatility control."
   b. Longer periods introduce a risk of pushing costs too far into the future and may also create **negative amortization** (no part of the principal balance is paid off).

One of the most helpful policies is to monitor the payment of principal each year.

Table 16 provides a sample of different payment schedules for paying down the UAL of a plan.

Table 16: Amortization Schedule for Paying Down UAL

Amortization Schedule Original Principal balance of $1,000,000 Assume a 10 year payment schedule									
Level Dollar Payment Amortization					Level percent of pay Amortization- payroll growth at 5%				
Year	Beginning of year principal amount	Total Payment	Interest at 7%	Principal Payment	Year	Beginning of year principal amount	Total Payment	Interest at 7%	Principal Payment
1	$ 1,000,000	$142,378	$ 70,000	$72,378	1	$ 1,000,000	$116,313	$ 70,000	$46,313
2	$ 927,622	$142,378	$ 64,934	$77,444	2	$ 953,687	$122,128	$ 66,758	$55,370
3	$ 850,179	$142,378	$ 59,512	$82,865	3	$ 898,317	$128,235	$ 62,882	$65,352
4	$ 767,314	$142,378	$ 53,712	$88,666	4	$ 832,965	$134,646	$ 58,308	$76,339
5	$ 678,648	$142,378	$ 47,505	$94,872	5	$ 756,626	$141,379	$ 52,964	$88,415
6	$ 583,776	$142,378	$ 40,864	$101,513	6	$ 668,211	$148,448	$ 46,775	$101,673
7	$ 482,263	$142,378	$ 33,758	$108,619	7	$ 566,538	$155,870	$ 39,658	$116,212
8	$ 373,644	$142,378	$ 26,155	$116,222	8	$ 450,326	$163,664	$ 31,523	$132,141
9	$ 257,421	$142,378	$ 18,019	$124,358	9	$ 318,185	$171,847	$ 22,273	$149,574
10	$ 133,063	$142,378	$ 9,314	$133,063	10	$ 168,612	$180,439	$ 11,803	$168,636
Total		$1,423,775	$ 423,775	$1,000,000	Total		$1,462,967	$ 462,943	$1,000,025

Table 16 illustrates the primary tenet that larger payments decrease long-term costs. The level dollar approach costs $1.4 million to pay off the original $1.0 million. The level percent of pay method costs $1.46 million in contributions to pay off the original $1.0 million.

Negative amortization generally occurs with level percent of pay funding over about 30 years.

Table 17 is an excerpt of an example showing negative amortization.

Table 17: Negative Amortization: 30-Year Period

Negative Amortization- 30 year period				
Year	Beginning of year principal amount	Total Payment	Interest at 7%	Principal Payment
1	$ 1,000,000	$46,272	$ 70,000	($23,728)
2	$ 1,023,728	$48,586	$ 71,661	($23,075)
3	$ 1,046,803	$51,015	$ 73,276	($22,261)
4	$ 1,069,064	$53,566	$ 74,834	($21,269)
5	$ 1,090,333	$56,244	$ 76,323	($20,079)
6	$ 1,110,412	$59,056	$ 77,729	($18,672)
7	$ 1,129,084	$62,009	$ 79,036	($17,027)
8	$ 1,146,111	$65,110	$ 80,228	($15,118)
9	$ 1,161,229	$68,365	$ 81,286	($12,921)
10	$ 1,174,150	$71,783	$ 82,190	($10,407)
...	...	...	...	...
Total		$582,007	$ 766,564	($184,557)

The principal balance continues to grow (thus the term negative amortization).

PART III

PRESENTING VALUATION RESULTS

9

The Policy Framework

Any funding policy will require tactics for successful implementation. A funding policy will lead to specific tactics for the assumptions and methods underlying the actuarial valuation. The valuation results are the expression of the funding policy. While it is a relatively simple message to communicate a required contribution, the deeper message may also include some additional facts such as:

- The promised benefits will be here when an employee retires
- The assumptions are built to last
- The contribution rate is constructed to be as stable as possible
- The plan is on a path to full funding (or not)
- The valuation report creates transparency on the funding strategy for the plan

When tying the plan and its actuarial practices to the overall policy for benefits and funding, you create a principles-based program rather than a benefit plan easily changed on a whim. Legislators and other decision-makers will realize a change in the plan's funding is also a change in policy. When decision-makers understand the funding policy, they can make decisions that fit into the overall objectives of the organization.

THE POLICY FRAMEWORK

The valuation process leads to the development of an actuarially-determined contribution. This process is derived from general policy objectives. The Conference of Consulting Actuaries Public Plans Community (CCA PPC) released a white paper in October 2014 outlining five major general policy objectives. These objectives provide the framework for the valuation process:

1. Future contributions and current plan assets should be sufficient to provide for all benefits expected to be paid to members and their beneficiaries when due.
2. The annual contribution should maintain a close relationship to the expected cost of each year of service.
3. Future contribution rate volatility should be controlled (i.e., costs emerge as a level percent of payroll) to the extent reasonably possible, consistent with other policy goals.
4. The general public policy goals of accountability and transparency are supported. Each element of the funding policy clarifies both as to intent and effect. The funding policy should allow an assessment of whether, how and when the plan sponsor is expected to meet the funding requirements of the plan.
5. The nature of public sector pension plans and their governance are considered in the funding policy. These governance issues include agency risk and a sustained budgeting commitment from plan sponsors. Agency risk issues include the desire of interested parties (agents) to influence the cost calculations.

To see how a funding method satisfies these policy objectives, think of a pie chart. The value of the pie is the value of all the benefits to be paid from the plan. Figure H depicts an example of this funding method.

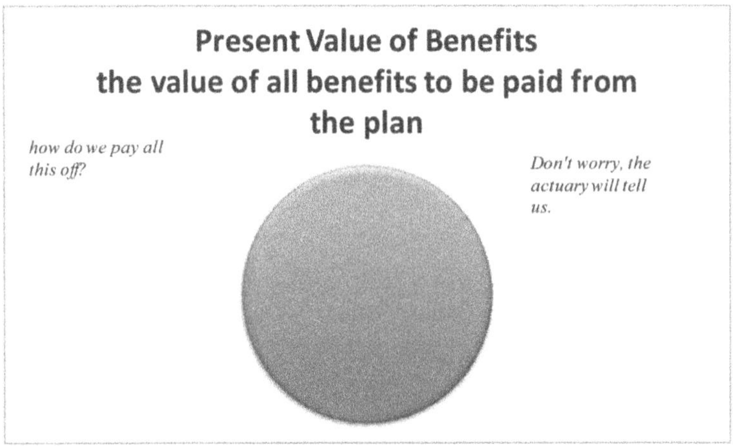

Figure H: Present Value of Benefits

The funding method splits this total value of benefits into two pieces: an accrued liability (for any benefits already earned) and future normal costs. This split is often referred to as a "timing" split because it is splitting the present value between past and future accruals. Figures I through K extend the data to show what may happen later.

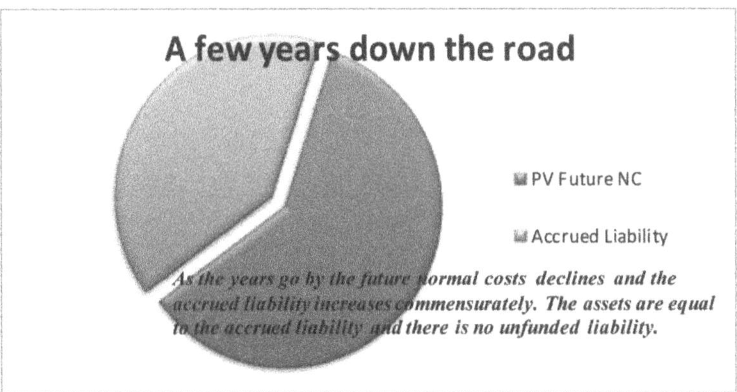

Figure I: Subsequent Accrued Liability and Future Normal Costs

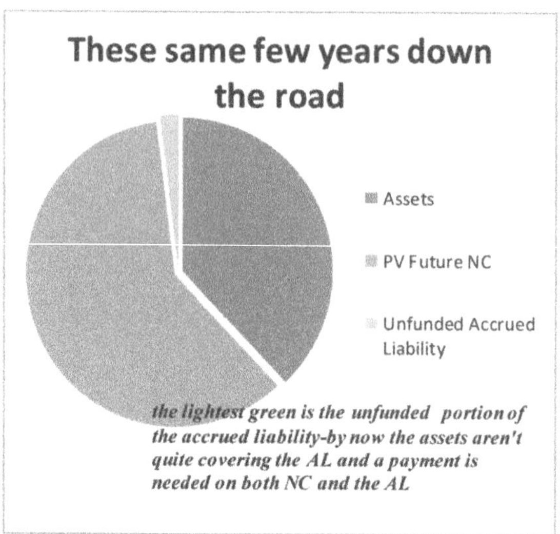

Figure J: Unfunded Portion of Accrued Liability versus Assets and Normal Costs

So many plans experienced the severe downturn in 2008 and 2009. Figure K shows how the unfunded portion of the accrued liability emerged (the medium green portion of the pie). When a UAL exists, payments on the UAL will be added to the actuarial determined contribution.

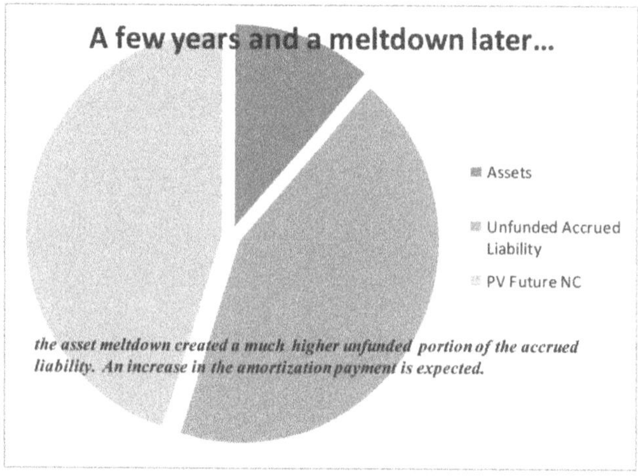

Figure K: Increased Unfunded Accrued Liability

The funding method accounts for the total pie (all benefits are valued) and creates recommended contributions on the unfunded parts of the pie (the normal cost and the amortization payments).

> *Future contributions and current plan assets should be sufficient to provide for all benefits expected to be paid to members and their beneficiaries when due.*

This objective is handled through the use of an acceptable actuarial funding method. In actuarial terms, this states the present value of all benefits to be paid is funded through the combination of contributions and investment earnings.

In reviewing the earlier CHAPTER: THE FUNDAMENTAL EQUATION OF BALANCE

All benefits must be valued; nothing can be left out.

The sum of future contributions and past contributions must equal the present value of all benefits.

The present value of all benefits must equal the present value of the future normal costs plus the accrued liability.

> *The annual contribution should maintain a close relationship to the expected cost of each year of service.*

This policy is achieved by using a funding method that develops an annual cost (a normal cost) that is developed by valuing the benefit accrual earned in the year of service. Paying off the UAL should relate to the population for which the UAL exists. For example, funding a retiree cost of living allowance (COLA) over 30 years would not be a match to the expected years of service for the group creating the UAL.

> *Future contribution rate volatility should be controlled (i.e., costs emerge as a level percent of payroll) to the extent reasonably possible, consistent with other policy goals.*

Contribution volatility is in the eye of the beholder. However, the funding method which develops the normal cost can be selected on the basis of either a flat dollar amount or a level percent of pay. Funding methods for both the normal cost and the UAL are selected by the fund's board. Sometimes, however, the funding method and/or assumptions may be set by statute. Either the flat dollar amount or level percent of pay method is chosen to determine the contribution to the retirement plan. The plan may choose a different funding method for the normal cost and the UAL payments.

Paying off the UAL can be done on either a level dollar amount or a level percent of pay amount. Other practices contribute to managing contribution rate volatility. For example, keeping assumptions updated will prevent the funding of the plan from hitting big bumps due to the erosion of the funded ratio.

> *The general public policy goals of accountability and transparency should be supported. Each element of the funding policy should be clear both as to intent and effect. The funding policy should allow an assessment of whether, how, and when the plan sponsor is expected to meet the funding requirements of the plan.*

This accountability and transparency is achieved through the development of a written funding policy. Once the terms of the funding policy are known, the valuation report and related communications are updated to tie directly to the funding policy.

The nature of public sector pension plans and their governance should be considered in the funding policy. These governance issues include (1) agency risk issues associated with the desire of interested parties (agents) to influence the cost calculations and (2) the need for a sustained budgeting commitment from plan sponsors.

A healthy plan sponsor supports a healthy plan. This funding policy objective helps support the health of the entire organization. It also recognizes the delicate balancing act between the plan sponsor and the plan. The funding policy may consider other items. These other items are a "rounding policy" or a "contribution reserve" policy. These policies are used to partner with the sponsor in coordinating with the budget.

10

Assumption Performance

ASSESSING THE ACTUARIAL ASSUMPTIONS

Each year trustees review the annual valuation report and ask, "What contributed to the changes from one year to the next? Why did the contribution rates change as they did? What were the biggest factors in the change in the contribution requirements?"

One fairly standard tool in the actuarial valuation report is the annual gain/loss by source. This tool looks at the accrued liability in the prior year and then measures the change contributed by each major assumption category. As a result, the valuation report shows how the mortality assumption fared in predicted longevity, or how the investment return assumption did meeting its goal.

A gain occurs when the liabilities perform better than expected, meaning costs are lower. This can occur when salaries are lower than expected. The lower salary implies a lower future retirement benefit since the ultimate benefit is based on final average compensation.

A gain occurs when people leave the plan (death or termination) sooner than expected. This creates a gain because a member leaving early means they are not accruing their full retirement benefit.

A loss occurs when a retiree lives a lot longer than expected. The loss is created because current retirees are receiving more benefits than anticipated.

Table 18 provides a sample exhibit of a gain/loss by source analysis ($ in millions).

Table 18: Gain/Loss by Source

Annual Change in Accrued Liability due to actual experience differing from assumed		
(Gain)-experience was favorable compared to assumptions (lowering the liability)		
Salary Increases	$6.70	*A loss here means salary increases were higher than assumed; those higher salaries translate into higher benefits*
Retirement	1.5	*This may mean more members retired with an early retirement subsidy than assumed; subsidies cost the plan*
Mortality	-2.6	*Gains on mortality mean more members died than were assumed-more deaths is the same as not living as long as expected*
Termination	4	*Members were staying in employment and earning more retirement benefits than assumed (not withdrawing)*
Disability	-0.6	*A few more disability retirements than assumed and disability benefits less valuable than the retirement benefits*
New entrants	2.8	*This is a usual and customary amount*
Other	3.7	*This is for all the items that are not in one of the major categories. The important point is to make sure it is NOT the largest item on the list*
Total	$15.40	*This says that the accrued liability increased from last year to this year, primarily due to salary increases higher than assumption and withdrawals slower than assumed!*

This annual analysis tells you how well assumptions are "meeting expectations." Large numbers in either direction will show a "miss" and smaller numbers indicate the valuation assumptions are more closely matching expectations. Note that one year's experience should not be used as a basis for a decision on the assumption. Actuaries will typically look at gains and losses over a multi-year period before recommending changes in assumptions.

A rule of thumb: Total demographic gain/loss ought to be less than 1% of the total accrued liabilities in a large plan. If it is greater than 1% (which implies some assumption was significantly off), it is time to review the assumptions with the actuary in greater detail. In a small plan one death could create a change in the accrued liability of more than 1%, so caution must be used in developing the "rule of thumb."

11

Peer Group: Assessing Where You Stand

Where do you stand among your "pension plan" peers?

Defining your peer group is an important first step in comparing one pension plan trust to another. Some key differences may make the comparisons more (or less) valid. For example, if your plan has a population excluded from Social Security then, when comparing benefits, select other non-Social Security plans. Public safety plans (police, fire, corrections) can be compared to other public safety plans.

Other plans also hire advisors and face similar decisions. A peer group comparison aids in contextualizing your plan's performance within the industry. The comparison also helps indicate if your plan has experienced something unusual. An outlier in returns, benefits, asset allocation, or any other metric can be worth exploring for its underlying policy and purpose.

Many peer group studies exist. These studies are frequently performed by associations. Some of the more commonly referenced associations are:

NASRA-National Association of State Retirement Administrators: Beginning with fiscal year 2001, the Public Fund Survey contains data on public retirement systems that provide pension and other benefits for 12.8 million active (working) members and 9.1 million retirees and beneficiaries. At the end of fiscal year 2016, plans in the Survey held combined assets of $3.16 trillion. The membership and assets of the plans included in the Survey comprise approximately 85 percent of the entire state and local government retirement system community. This survey can be found at www.NASRA.org

NCTR-National Council on Teacher Retirement: NCTR membership includes 68 state, territorial, and local pension systems. These systems serve more than 19 million active and retired teachers, non-teaching personnel, and other public employees; and have combined assets of over $2 trillion in their trust funds. Further information can be found at www.nctr.org

NCPERS-National Conference on Public Employee Retirement Systems: The National Conference on Public Employee Retirement Systems (NCPERS) is the largest trade association for public sector pension funds, representing more than 500 funds throughout the United States and Canada. It is a unique non-profit network of trustees, administrators, public officials and investment professionals. Collectively they manage nearly $3 trillion in pension assets held in trust for approximately 21 million public employees and retirees—including firefighters, law enforcement officers, teachers, and other public servants. Further information can be found at www.ncpers.org.

Tables 19a-d provide the assumed rates of returns for 2016/2017 (96 plans) and related targets (89 plans).

Table 19a: Assumed Rates of Returns

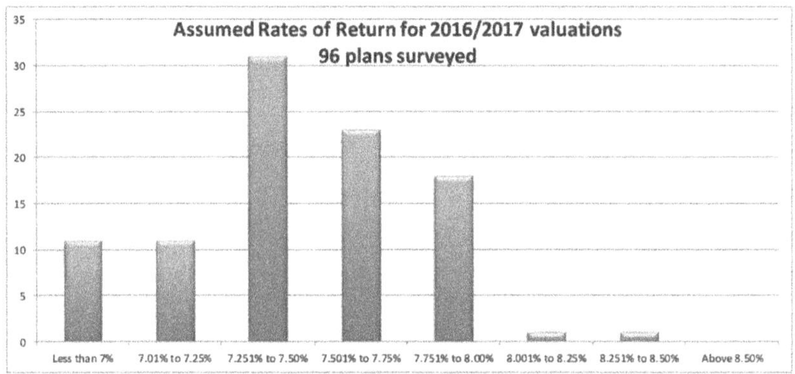

Table 19b: Assumed Rates of Returns

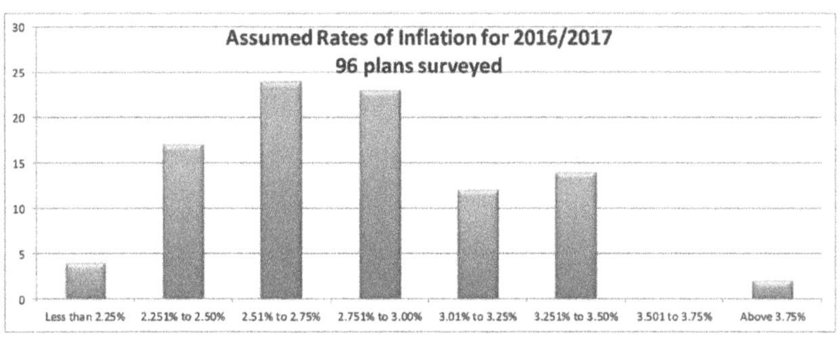

Table 19c: Targeted Equity Allocation

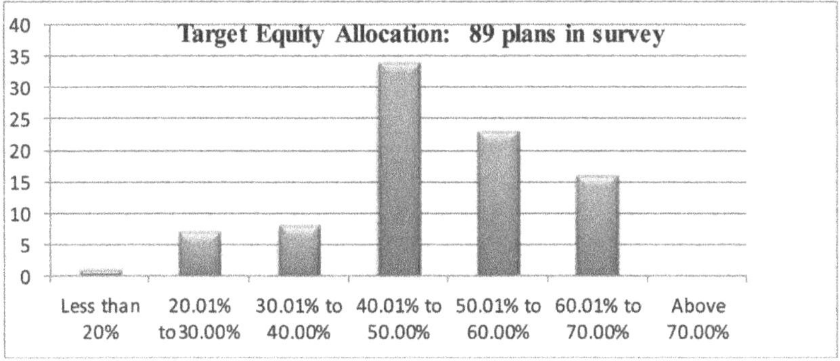

Table 19d: Target Alternative Allocation

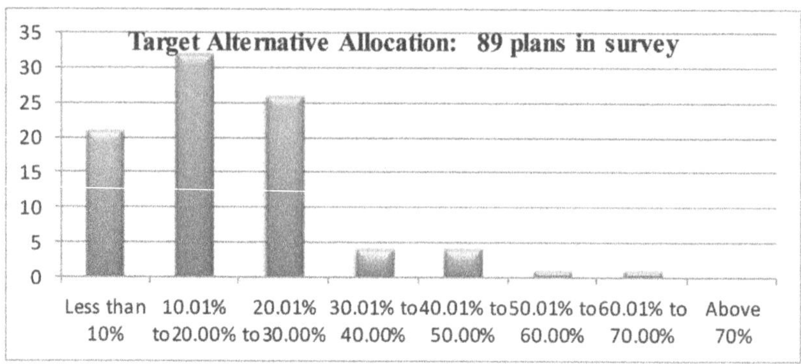

PART IV

LOOKING INTO THE FUTURE

LOOKING INTO THE FUTURE

A valuation is only a snapshot in time of the actuarial condition of a plan. Time is also a major factor in both the accrual of benefits (benefits accrue as time passes) and the funding of the plan (assets grow as time passes). Time can be thought of as a resource for funding. Decision-makers use projections to monitor the funding direction of the plan.

Projections provide results that are directional, not precise. The farther out the future is projected, the less certainty exists for that future. That is an inherent feature of predictions. However, projections can inform you of the potential outcomes in the future and the various levels of sensitivity to certain inputs that a future state of your plan may have.

Missing the actuarial assumption in one year has a significant impact on the funded ratio 30 years into the future. This should not precipitate a knee-jerk reaction today. Rather, knowing how sensitive the plan is helps you to see how soon you need to make a decision about your assumptions.

The next chapter looks at how projections are built. The chapter illustrates what to watch out for when looking into the future of the funding of your organization's retirement plan.

12

Leading Indicators and Outcomes

What is the desired outcome of a pension plan? Boards wrestle regularly with this question, since there are many answers to what the board and plan sponsor are seeking. But all would agree one of the critical desired outcomes is for the plan to pay all benefits when due.

A great example of a leading indicator and a desired outcome is weight loss. The weight loss itself is an outcome. The leading indicators could be calories ingested and calories burned. The leading indicators will give us a good idea, before weighing in, whether the outcome will be as desired.

Let's start with the desired outcome of paying all benefits when due. Leading indicators would be those metrics measurable today but illustrating a trend toward (or away from) the desired outcome. A leading indicator that shows the desired outcome will be met could be the annual required contribution is met. Another leading indicator could be the outstanding balance on the UAL is declining.

Table 20 provides some samples of leading indicators.

Table 20: Samples of Leading Indicators

Samples of Leading Indicators	*Outcome*
The Actuarially Determined Contribution (ADC) is always paid	Plan will always have assets to cover benefit payments.
The balance of the unfunded accrued liability is growing every year	Indicates contributions will need to increase; run projection to test whether assets will be depleted if the ADC cannot be made.
The interest rate assumption has not been met over a long period	Indicates assumption made need revisions, implying the liabilities and costs are not adequate to cover the contribution requirements. Run projection to test whether the change in assumptions still generates an ADC that can be made and whether assets will be fully depleted.
The market value of assets is lower than the actuarial value of assets	Indicates losses from prior years will still be "smoothed into" the actuarial value of assets. This creates upward pressure on the contribution rate. The reverse is true when the market value of assets is higher than the actuarial value of assets.

Caution must be exercised when working with these metrics. Facts are facts, but the conclusion drawn from the facts may be in error.

For example, you may know the assets only earned 1% for the prior year while the plan's assumed rate of return is 7%. In spite of the loss on the assets, the actuary says the funded ratio increased!

The leading indicator is both the increase in the funded ratio and the asset returns not meeting the assumed rate. How can assets only earn 1% and the plan still experience an increase in the funded ratio?

First, the asset returns for each year are being smoothed over a period (most typically five years). There may be gains on the investments within the last five years being recognized today. Even though the market value return was 1%, the actuarial value of assets may have returned 8%. Drawing the conclusion that the plan is "trending down" when the assumed interest rate was not met would be erroneous.

It is always prudent to look at a 30-year projection of your plan's actuarial metrics. This tells you the projected outcome over the 30- year period based on the assumptions used in your plan.

13

Understanding Where the Plan is Headed

Table 21 is a basis of actuarial projections. This table gives you assistance in understanding how to assess the health and direct of your plan's assets.

Table 21: Actuarial Projection Basis

The Basics of Actuarial Projections							
			Liabilities		Contributions		
Year	Payroll (000's)*	Assets**	Accrued Liability***	Unfunded Accrued Liability	Normal Cost	UAL payment	Actuarially Det. Contribution (ADC)
2020	$1,000	$5,000	$5,000	$0	$120	$0	$120
2021	$1,030	$5,478	$5,478	$0	$124	$0	$124
2022	$1,061	$5,994	$5,994	$0	$127	$0	$127
2023	$1,093	$6,550	$6,550	$0	$131	$0	$131
2024	$1,126	$7,149	$7,149	$0	$135	$0	$135

* assumes 3% payroll growth per year.
** assets increase by the ARC and 7% assumed rate of return.
*** the accrued liability increases by normal cost and decreases by benefit payments (which are assumed to be zero).
UAL payment based on 7% assumed rate of return; 20 year open amortization.

Table 20 is a scaled-down version of a projection. Now we will look at each main element of the projection model to give you an idea how these pieces all fit together. Then we will return to this example to see how to interpret the results.

First, the total payroll for the entire population is projected. In this simplified example you can take each year's payroll, multiply it by 1.03 (for the 3% payroll growth assumption) and you will then have the projected value of next year's payroll. Table 22 provides a summary of the projected payroll in this example.

Table 22: Projected Payroll

Projected Payroll								
			Liabilities		Contributions			
Year	Payroll (000's)*	Assets**	Accrued Liability***	Unfunded Accrued Liability	Normal Cost	UAL payment	Actuarially Det. Contribution (ADC)
2020	$1,000	$5,000	$5,000	$0	$120	$0	$120
2021	$1,030	$5,478	$5,478	$0	$124	$0	$124
2022	$1,061	$5,994	$5,994	$0	$127	$0	$127
2023	$1,093	$6,550	$6,550	$0	$131	$0	$131
2024	$1,126	$7,149	$7,149	$0	$135	$0	$135

Payroll grows each year by the assumed growth in payroll.

In this case payroll is assumed to grow at 3% per year.
Total payroll will change as members retire,others are hired, and ongoing members receive raises.

Next let's project assets. The value of your trust's assets is a little more complicated. First, contributions are added to the trust assets, benefit payments and expenses are subtracted, and then the investment earnings are added to the total value of the trust. For simplicity, this example assumed the ADC was made on the first day of the year. There are no benefit payments in this example. Thus, you take the assets plus the ADC and multiply the total by 7% to account for the 7% assumed rate of return. That total, which is $358, is added to the $5,120 for the ending balance of $5,478. Table 23 shows the projected assets for this example.

Table 23: Projected Assets

Projected Assets								
			Liabilities		Contributions		
Year	Payroll (000's)*	Assets**	Accrued Liability***	Unfunded Accrued Liability	Normal Cost	UAL payment	Actuarially Det. Contribution (ADC)
2020	$1,000	$5,000	$5,000	$0	$120	$0	$120
2021	$1,030	$5,478	$5,478	$0	$124	$0	$124
2022	$1,061	$5,994	$5,994	$0	$127	$0	$127
2023	$1,093	$6,550	$6,550	$0	$131	$0	$131
2024	$1,126	$7,149	$7,149	$0	$135	$0	$135

Assets are projected by adding in the annual required contribution, subtracting benefit payments and adjusting for a 7% assumed rate of return.

In this example there are no benefit payments.

Next, let's look at how the accrued liability is projected. The accrued liability moves forward by adding the normal cost and subtracting the benefit payments, and the result is adjusted using the assumed rate of return. This example is a simplified since the normal cost is equal to the annual required contribution. Table 24 shows the projected accrued liability for our example.

Table 24: Projected Accrued Liability

Projected Accrued Liability							
			Liabilities		Contributions		
Year	Payroll (000's)*	Assets**	Accrued Liability***	Unfunded Accrued Liability	Normal Cost	UAL payment	Actuarially Det. Contribution (ADC)
2020	$1,000	$5,000	$5,000	$0	$120	$0	$120
2021	$1,030	$5,478	$5,478	$0	$124	$0	$124
2022	$1,061	$5,994	$5,994	$0	$127	$0	$127
2023	$1,093	$6,550	$6,550	$0	$131	$0	$131
2024	$1,126	$7,149	$7,149	$0	$135	$0	$135

The accrued liability increases each year by adding normal cost, subtracting benefit payments and adjusting for the assumed rate of return.
The accrued liability is the accumulated value of past normal costs.
When assets equal the accrued liability then all those past normal costs are "covered" and the plan is "fully funded".

The UAL is the difference between the accrued liability and the assets. In this example, the accrued liability and the assets are always equal (because the ADC is always made and the assumptions are always met). The UAL stays at zero, implying the plan is 100% (fully) funded in all those years. Tables 25a-b show the projected UAL and the projected normal cost for this example.

Table 25a: Projected Unfunded Accrued Liability

Projected Unfunded Accrued Liability							
		Liabilities			Contributions		
Year	Payroll (000's)*	Assets**	Accrued Liability***	**Unfunded Accrued Liability**	Normal Cost	UAL payment	Actuarially Det. Contribution (ADC)
2020	$1,000	$5,000	$5,000	**$0**	$120	$0	$120
2021	$1,030	$5,478	$5,478	**$0**	$124	$0	$124
2022	$1,061	$5,994	$5,994	**$0**	$127	$0	$127
2023	$1,093	$6,550	$6,550	**$0**	$131	$0	$131
2024	$1,126	$7,149	$7,149	**$0**	$135	$0	$135

The unfunded accrued liability is the difference between the assets and the accrued liability.

Table 25b: Projected Normal Cost

Projected Normal Cost							
		Liabilities			Contributions		
Year	Payroll (000's)*	Assets**	Accrued Liability***	Unfunded Accrued Liability	**Normal Cost**	UAL payment	Actuarially Det. Contribution (ADC)
2020	$1,000	$5,000	$5,000	$0	**$120**	$0	$120
2021	$1,030	$5,478	$5,478	$0	**$124**	$0	$124
2022	$1,061	$5,994	$5,994	$0	**$127**	$0	$127
2023	$1,093	$6,550	$6,550	$0	**$131**	$0	$131
2024	$1,126	$7,149	$7,149	$0	**$135**	$0	$135

The normal cost is the annual cost for the annual accrual of benefits.

The funding method used will dictate how the normal cost is calculated.

This method develops a normal cost that is 12% of payroll.

The funding method works to achieve a normal cost that is constant as a percent of payroll. In this example the assumption keeps the normal cost at 12% of payroll. To determine each year's normal cost, take the payroll number and multiply it by 0.12. It is interesting to note the normal cost is the same 12% of payroll year over year, but it increases in dollar amount each year. In fact, the normal cost will increase at the same rate as payroll growth (which our examples assumed to be 3% per year).

However, normal cost is only half of the contribution story. Whenever an unfunded liability exists, a payment on the UAL must be made. This example maintains a $0 UAL, so the payment amount is $0. Table 26 shows the projected UAL payment for our example.

Table 26: Projected UAL Payment

Projected UAL Payment							
			Liabilities		Contributions		
Year	Payroll (000's)*	Assets**	Accrued Liability***	Unfunded Accrued Liability	Normal Cost	UAL payment	Actuarially Det. Contribution (ADC)
2020	$1,000	$5,000	$5,000	$0	$120	$0	$120
2021	$1,030	$5,478	$5,478	$0	$124	$0	$124
2022	$1,061	$5,994	$5,994	$0	$127	$0	$127
2023	$1,093	$6,550	$6,550	$0	$131	$0	$131
2024	$1,126	$7,149	$7,149	$0	$135	$0	$135

The UAL payment is the annual payment on the unfunded accrued liability based on the funding policy.
In this case the amortization payment is based on level dollar, 20 year open amortization (were it not zero!)

Finally, the projection model will add the Normal Cost and the UAL payment to determine the ADC. This is depicted in Table 27.

Table 27: Projected Annual Required Contribution

Projected Annual Required Contribution							
		Liabilities			Contributions		
Year	Payroll (000's)*	Assets**	Accrued Liability***	Unfunded Accrued Liability	Normal Cost	UAL payment	Actuarially Det. Contribution (ADC)
2020	$1,000	$5,000	$5,000	$0	$120	$0	$120
2021	$1,030	$5,478	$5,478	$0	$124	$0	$124
2022	$1,061	$5,994	$5,994	$0	$127	$0	$127
2023	$1,093	$6,550	$6,550	$0	$131	$0	$131
2024	$1,126	$7,149	$7,149	$0	$135	$0	$135

The actuarially determined contribution is the sum of the normal cost and the UAL payment.

Now let's put the entire projection together under a few different scenarios and see what conclusions may be drawn. This first projection scenario represents the idyllic world of perpetual full funding.

In Table 28, the left side of the chart illustrates the development of the assets and liabilities; the right side translates those amounts into the contribution requirements.

Table 28: The Perfect World of Staying Fully Funded

The Perfect World of Staying Fully Funded										
Liabilities					Contributions					
Year	Payroll (000's)*	Assets**	Accrued Liability***	Unfunded Accrued Liability	Year	Payroll (000's)*	Normal Cost	UAL payment	Actuarially Det. Contribution (ADC)
2020	$1,000	$5,000	$5,000	$0	2020	$1,000	$120	$0	$120
2021	$1,030	$5,478	$5,478	$0	2021	$1,030	$124	$0	$124
2022	$1,061	$5,994	$5,994	$0	2022	$1,061	$127	$0	$127
2023	$1,093	$6,550	$6,550	$0	2023	$1,093	$131	$0	$131
2024	$1,126	$7,149	$7,149	$0	2024	$1,126	$135	$0	$135

* assumes 3% payroll growth per year
** assets increase by the ARC and 7% assumed rate of return
*** the accrued liability increases by normal cost and decreases by benefit payments (which are assumed to be zero)
UAL payment based on 7% assumed rate of return, 20 year open amortization

This is the "perfect" scenario where the plan has zero unfunded liabilities UALs year after year. The annual required contribution is the normal cost each year-since no UAL exists. This plan has stayed current on all its normal cost contributions and has had no gains or losses impacting the accrued liability.

But pension plans are rarely perfect. Table 29 demonstrates the more likely situation for pension plans.

Table 29: The Not-So-Perfect World of having an Unfunded Accrued Liability

The Not-So-Perfect World of having an Unfunded Accrued Liability									
Liabilities						Contributions			
Year	Payroll (000's)*	Assets**	Accrued Liability***	Unfunded Accrued Liability	Year	Payroll (000's)*	Normal Cost	UAL payment	Actuarially Det. Contribution (ADC)
2020	$1,000	$5,000	$7,000	$2,000	2020	$1,000	$120	$189	$309
2021	$1,030	$5,680	$7,618	$1,938	2021	$1,030	$124	$183	$307
2022	$1,061	$6,406	$8,284	$1,878	2022	$1,061	$127	$177	$305
2023	$1,093	$7,180	$9,000	$1,820	2023	$1,093	$131	$172	$303
2024	$1,126	$8,007	$9,770	$1,763	2024	$1,126	$135	$166	$302

* assumes 3% payroll growth per year
** assets increase by the ARC and 7% assumed rate of return
*** the accrued liability increases by normal cost and decreases by benefit payments
UAL payment based on 7% assumed rate of return, 20 year open amortization

Here is Table 30, showing a projection with a UAL. The annual required payments now include the normal cost plus a payment on the UAL. As the UAL decreases, so do the UAL payments.

Table 30: The World of Negative Cash Flow

The World of Negative Cash Flow (benefit payments greater than contributions)									
Liabilities					Contributions				
Year	Payroll (000's)*	Assets**	Accrued Liability***	Unfunded Accrued Liability	Year	Payroll (000's)*	Normal Cost	UAL payment	Actuarially Det. Contribution (ADC)
2020	$1,000	$5,000	$7,000	$2,000	2020	$1,000	$120	$189	$309
2021	$1,030	$5,145	$7,083	$1,938	2021	$1,030	$124	$183	$307
2022	$1,061	$5,266	$7,144	$1,878	2022	$1,061	$127	$177	$305
2023	$1,093	$5,360	$7,180	$1,820	2023	$1,093	$131	$172	$303
2024	$1,126	$5,422	$7,185	$1,763	2024	$1,126	$135	$166	$302

* assumes 3% payroll growth per year
** assets increase by the ARC and 7% assumed rate of return
*** the accrued liability increases by normal cost and decreases by benefit payments
UAL payment based on 7% assumed rate of return, 20 year open amortization
Annual Benefit payments asumed are: $500; $530; $562; $596 and $631

Next, let's look at a case which includes benefit payments. In fact, in our example, the outflow of benefit payments exceeds the inflow of contributions.

How interesting…the assets and the accrued liability differ, but the ADC matches the previous example!

This is because the accrued liability and the assets are decreasing by the same amount: the amount of the benefit payments. That creates an equal unfunded amount as in the previous example.

But beware! Negative cash flow is bringing the assets down. In the earlier example, assets were rising to $8,007 while the introduction of the benefit payments brings the assets to $5,422.

It is important to NOT conclude features like lump sum cashouts can help the plan. The issue needs examination.

In fact, let's look at what happens with "a run on the plan." Table 31 shows the impact of a "super" negative cash flow on the pension plan in our example.

Table 31: The World of Super-Negative Cash Flow

The World of Super Negative Cash Flow (benefit payments greater than contributions)									
Liabilities					Contributions				
Year	Payroll (000's)*	Assets**	Accrued Liability***	Unfunded Accrued Liability	Year	Payroll (000's)*	Normal Cost	UAL payment	Actuarially Det. Contribution (ADC)
2020	$1,000	$5,000	$7,000	$2,000	2020	$1,000	$120	$189	$309
2021	$1,030	$3,540	$5,478	$1,938	2021	$1,030	$124	$183	$307
2022	$1,061	$1,848	$3,726	$1,878	2022	$1,061	$127	$177	$305
2023	$1,093	-$101	$1,718	$1,718	2023	$1,093	$131	$162	$293
2024	$1,126	-$330	$1,444	$1,444	2024	$1,126	$135	$136	$271

* assumes 3% payroll growth per year
** assets increase by the ARC and 7% assumed rate of return
*** the accrued liability increases by normal cost and decreases by benefit payments
UAL payment based on 7% assumed rate of return, 20 year open amortization
Annual benefit payments assumed are: $2,000; $2,120; $2,247;$500;0

The plan runs out of money within three years: a very short period of time. The plan would not be able to invest the assets to produce the needed returns within the required time period.

Projections help all interested parties see the anticipated path for the retirement plan. The projection is only as good as the assumptions regarding future experience. Projections are most often directional rather than precise due to the very nature of attempting to predict the future. All plans should conduct projections to gain an understanding of the probable future path of the plan. These projections focus on the sensitivity of the plan to variations in key assumptions.

ASKING QUESTIONS

Keep a list of questions handy to ask the actuary. Here are some questions to get you started. These questions are organized by the primary categories of the actuarial valuation report.

ASSUMPTIONS

Do you see any assumptions not performing well?
Do you see any assumptions requiring a change?
Which assumptions have the greatest impact on the plan?
When do we need to change assumptions?

DATA

Did you see anything unusual in the data?
Were there more retirements/deaths/terminations/disabilities than expected?

ASSETS

What is the smoothing method?
How is the smoothing method working?
Are we expecting gains or losses in the future?
Do expenses seem out of line?
Did any aspect of the assets appear to be an outlier?

NORMAL COST

Has the plan's objective to fund current normal cost been met? (Whether level dollar or level percent of pay)?

If there are benefits based on a member's hire date, are those benefits reducing the normal cost as new entrants join the plan?

ACCRUED LIABILITY

What were the significant sources of change in the accrued liability?
How much did the accrued liability change due to assumption/benefit/experience?

UNFUNDED ACCRUED LIABILITY

Did principal get paid off?
Is the plan experiencing negative amortization?
If negative amortization is occurring how long is it expected to last?
What were the biggest contributors to the change in the UAL from last year?

14

Distinguishing the Important From the Urgent: Actuarial Metrics

Employers with well-funded retirement plans take a long-term approach to looking at the sustainability and affordability of the retirement system. This long-term look makes it difficult to know precisely when a situation warrants immediate action. In a checking account, for example, a notification from the bank of insufficient funds requires immediate action. In a pension plan, the existence of an UAL may not require any additional actions beyond the status quo. That is the fundamental difference between an immediate cash flow and a long-term liability structure.

Actuarial valuation reports are full of many metrics, numbers, and conclusions. Difficulty exists sorting through the various statistics presented by the actuarial report. Determining what course of action to take and how soon the action is required is challenging. This CHAPTER lays out ideas to help you discern what may require immediate action. Then you can decide which, if any actions, need to take place. As a trustee, you and your fellow trustees must decide what may be important to consider but not require immediate action, and what does not require action at this time.

To frame the discussion, we will use Table 32, which is a 2 by 2 table: an "important and urgent" table.

Table 32: An "Important and Urgent" 2 by 2 Matrix

	Not Important	Important (policy infraction)	
Urgent (cost to waiting)	Requires action – not a violation of policy but has a cost (not always purely monetary) if not handled	**Requires Immediate Action**	Urgent (monetary or other costs to waiting)
Not Urgent	This would be benign measures: interesting facts not requiring any action	**Requires Action in the future**	Not Urgent
	Not Important	Important	

Each plan and board will set its own level of urgency around issues. Legislative pressures, board policy and broader policy concerns set the stage for the level of responsiveness for any given issue. However, as a starting point you may wish to consider the following:

A matter is ***urgent*** when there is a significant cost to waiting to take action. A matter could also be urgent if there is an undesirable penalty (i.e. the auditor will issue a qualified financial statement report unless a matter is handled; the IRS will assess penalties etc.).

A matter is ***important*** when it is out of alignment with known policies (i.e. policy requires an asset liability study every five years and the last one done was six years ago). A matter may be important when expectations are not met (such as actuarial assumptions).

Some examples are:

1. Asset returns for the year did not meet the assumed rate of return (important but not urgent)
2. The ratio of the assets to the accrued liability falls to less than 80% (important but not urgent)
3. The funded ratio has been declining for a number of years and is projected to continue to decline (important and urgent)
4. The number of retirees is increasing (not important and not urgent)
5. The actuarially determined contribution has not been made for any of the last 10 years (important and urgent)
6. The trust is expected to run out of funds in 10 years (important and urgent)
7. The principal amount on the unfunded accrued liability grew, rather than decreasing-known as negative amortization (important, not urgent)
8. The average age of new hires is increasing (not important, not urgent)
9. Staff forgot to post the valuation on the website (policy requires posting) (important and not urgent)
10. The member census shows a new retiree's spouse and future beneficiary is 15 years younger than the member. (important and not urgent).

Table 33 revisits the format and discussion in Table 32, but tailors the data to the preceding listed items.

Table 33: Tailored "Important and Urgent" Matrix

	Not Important	Important (policy infraction)	
Urgent (cost to waiting)	Trustees want to get the early bird rates for conference registration	**Funded ratio has been declining for years. Funded ratio expected to continue to decline. The ARC has not been made for 10 years. The trust is expected to run out of money in 10 years.**	Urgent (cost to waiting)
Not Urgent	The number of retirees is increasing. The average age of new hires is increasing.	**Asset returns for the current year did not meet the assumed rate. Funded ratio dropped below 80%. The principal balance on the UAL grew.**	Not Urgent
	Not Important	Important (policy infraction)	

Distinguishing the important from the urgent helps trustees determine what actions (e.g. further studies, plan design issues, assumption and method issues) are to be taken immediately, and what actions ought to be put on a "watch" list.

When working through the actuarial report and sifting through the findings, it is useful to ask the following:

1. What is the impact to the plan of waiting to take action on this matter?
2. How will the actuarial status of the plan look in 30 years if no action is taken?
3. What is the risk to the plan, to the members, and to the taxpayers if no action is ever taken on this matter?

Conclusion

This book serves as a reference to assist your journey through the maze of decisions trustees face annually. This book covers the basic components of an actuarial valuation. When trustees understand the components of the actuarial valuation they make informed decisions. They understand how changes to one component impact the results

As fiduciaries, balancing the competing obligations is continually challenged. You may not have a crystal ball, but you do have

A PENCHANT FOR PENSIONS

Reference Materials

Governing Bodies and Associations Glossary

GOVERNING ORGANIZATIONS

There is no single body governing public sector retirement plans. There are a number of places where there is governance concerning the practices of those professionals involved with the retirement plan.

ACTUARIAL BODIES

SOCIETY OF ACTUARIES WWW.SOA.ORG credentialed actuaries are members of the Society. The credentials are the ASA (Associate of the Society of Actuaries) and FSA (Fellow of the Society of Actuaries). Fellows have completed all the exams for their given specialty. Associates have completed some, but not all the exams.

AMERICAN ACADEMY OF ACTUARIES WWW.ACTUARY.ORG The American Academy of Actuaries, also known as the "Academy" or the AAA, is the body that represents and unites United States actuaries in all practice areas.

CONFERENCE OF CONSULTING ACTUARIES WWW.CCACTUARIES.ORG The Conference of Consulting Actuaries, also known as the Conference or the CCA, is a professional society of actuaries engaged in consulting in the United States and Canada, as opposed to those employed by insurance companies.

ACCOUNTING ORGANIZATIONS

GOVERNMENT ACCOUNTING STANDARDS BOARD (GASB) WWW.GASB.ORG The Governmental Accounting Standards Board is the source of generally accepted accounting principles used by state and local governments in the United States.

GOVERNMENT FINANCE OFFICERS ASSOCIATION (GFOA) WWW.GFOA.ORG The Government Finance Officers Association is a professional association of approximately 18,500 state, provincial, and local government finance officers in the United States and Canada.

PUBLIC PENSION ASSOCIATIONS

NATIONAL ASSOCIATION OF STATE RETIREMENT ADMINISTRATORS WWW.NASRA.ORG NASRA is a non-profit association whose members are the directors of the nation's state, territorial, and largest statewide public retirement systems. NASRA members oversee retirement systems that hold more than two-thirds of the $4.2 trillion held in trust for nearly 15 million working and 10 million retired employees of state and local government.

NCTR-NATIONAL COUNCIL ON TEACHER RETIREMENT WWW.NCTR.ORG NCTR membership includes 68 state, territorial, and local pension systems. These systems serve more than 19 million active and retired teachers, non-teaching personnel, and other public employees; and have combined assets of over $2 trillion in their trust funds.

NCPERS-NATIONAL CONFERENCE ON PUBLIC EMPLOYEE RETIREMENT SYSTEMS WWW.NCPERS.ORG The National Conference on Public Employee Retirement Systems (NCPERS) is the largest trade association for public sector pension funds, representing more than 500 funds throughout the United States and Canada. It is a unique non-profit network of trustees, administrators, public officials and investment professionals who collectively manage nearly $3 trillion in pension assets held in trust for approximately 21 million public employees and retirees — including firefighters, law enforcement officers, teachers, and other public servants.

Glossary and Acronym List

A

AAA – The American Academy of Actuaries

Actuarial Determined Contribution (ADC) – An annual contribution amount developed by the actuary using generally accepted actuarial methods. The ADC is generally the sum of the normal cost and the payment on the unfunded accrued liability.

Accrued Liability – The plan's liability for promised benefit based on members' service to date.

AF – An accredited fiduciary issued by the National Conference of Public Employee Retirement Systems. This credential is awarded on the basis of an exam and experience on a public pension fund board.

Alternative Investments – Investments in private equity, hedge funds, managed futures, real estate commodities and derivative contracts.

Amortization – Paying off an amount over time by making planned incremental payments of principal and interest. A debt is "fully amortized" when the debt is paid off.

B

Balance Sheet – A statement of the assets, liabilities and capital of a business or other organization at a particular point in time.

Basis Point – One hundredth of one percent. Commonly used with investment return rates and expenses.

C

Capital Asset Pricing Model (CAPM) – An economic model that describes the relationship between systematic risk and expected return for assets, particularly stocks.

Capital Market – Markets for buying and selling equity and debt instruments.

Commodities – A raw material or primary agricultural product that can be bought and sold. Examples include gold or pork.

Conference of Consulting Actuaries (CCA) – A professional society of actuaries engaged in consulting in the United States and Canada, as opposed to those employed by insurance companies.

Conference of Consulting Actuaries Public Plan Community (CCA-PPC) – A subgroup within the Conference of Consulting Actuaries with members that focus on the public sector such as states cities, counties and public safety retirement plans.

Consumer Price Index (CPI) – Calculated by the US Department of labor Statistic's Bureau of Labor Statistics. This is a measure of the increase in prices for a given basket of goods.

Consumer Price Index – U: Consumer Price Index – U is Consumer Price Index of all Urban Consumers. This index includes all professional, self-employed individuals, retirees, clerical workers and others receiving regular income.

Consumer Price Index – W: W is the Consumer Price Index of urban wage earners and clerical workers. This index has been computed since 1913. This index represents 28% of the population.

Core Investments – Investments such as bonds, stocks and real estate holdings.

D

Demographic – This relates to populations. In the actuarial valuation this is an assumption about what happens to people (death, retirement, etc.) as opposed to an assumption about the economy.

E

EA – An actuarial designation for Enrolled Actuary under ERISA. This credential is awarded on the basis of exam and experience by the Joint Board for the Enrollment of Actuaries.

Emerging Markets – An economy that is advancing. Indicators of advancement include some liquidity in local debt and equity markets and the existence of some form of market exchange and regulatory body.

Entry Age Normal Funding Method – Under this funding method, the normal cost of each individual's pension is calculated as a level (dollar or percent of pay) amount between the time employment starts (entry age) and the assumed retirement date.

Equities – Shares of stock on a stock market held by individuals and firms in anticipation of income from dividends and capital gains.

ERISA – The Employee Retirement Income Security Act of 1974 (ERISA) enacted September 2, 1974 is a federal law that establishes minimum standards for pension plans in the private sector. The law provides for extensive rules on the federal income tax effects of transactions associated with employee benefit plans.

F

FCA – An actuarial designation for membership in the Conference of Consulting Actuaries. A Fellow of the Conference of Consulting Actuaries.

Federal Reserve – The United States Central Bank based in Washington, DC. It was created by Congress to provide the nation with a safe, more flexible and more stable monetary and financial system.

Federal Open Market Committee – The Federal Reserve's monetary policymaking board. Comprised of 12 members. All seven (7) of the Board of Governors and five (5) of the 12 Bank presidents. The five bank presidents rotate one-year terms.

Fixed Income – Includes corporate and municipal bonds. Refers to any type of investment under which the borrower or issuer is obliged to make payments of a fixed amount on a fixed schedule.

FSA – An actuarial designation for membership in the Society of Actuaries. This designation shows all actuarial exams were successfully completed. This is a Fellow of the Society of Actuaries.

G

GASB – Governmental Accounting Standards Board. The Board is a private not-for-profit organization that seeks to establish and improve the standards of accounting and financial reporting for U.S. state and local governments.

H

Hedge Fund – A limited partnership of investors that uses high risk methods. Investments such as investing with borrowed money in the hopes of realizing large capital gains.

I

Income and Expense Statement – An income statement is a financial statement that reports financial performance over a specified ccounting period. Financial performance is assessed by giving a summary of how the business incurs its revenue and expenses through both operating and non-operating activities.

Indexed US Treasury Bond – Treasury Bonds that include inflation or deflation as calculated by the CPI.

Inflation – The increase in prices of goods and services over time. A dollar tomorrow will buy less than today.

Inflation Indexed Security – A security that guarantees a rate of return higher than inflation when held to maturity.

Inflation Risk Premium – Rate of return in excess of the risk-free rate. Compensation to the investor for bearing additional risk.

M

Management - Active – Refers to a portfolio investment strategy where the manager makes specific investments with the goal of outperforming an investment benchmark.

Management - Passive – An investment strategy that mimics an externally managed index such as Dow Jones Index.

Modern Portfolio Theory – An hypothesis, by Henry Markowitz, that risk averse investors can construct portfolios to optimize returns based upon a given level of risk.

N

Negative Amortization – An increase in the principal balance of a loan caused by making payments that fail to cover the interest due. The remaining amount of interest owed is added to the loan's principal, which ultimately causes the borrower to owe more money.

Normal Cost – The value of the current year pension benefit accrual.

O

Other Post Employment Benefits (OPEB) – Non-retirement benefits payable to retirees. Examples include retiree health care, retiree dental benefits, retiree life insurance.

P

Payroll growth – Amount aggregate payroll increases each year.

Pay Status – The retiree or his or her beneficiary are receiving payments from the pension plan.

Percentile – Percentile usually indicates a certain percentage falls below that percentile.

Personal Consumption Expenditure – The primary measure of personal consumption of products and services by individuals. Experts project two-thirds of domestic spending comes from personal expenditures.

Private Markets – Investments not traded on a public exchange. This includes equity or fixed income investments placed directly into private companies.

Private Real Estate – An asset class consisting of pooled private and public investments in the real property markets.

Projected Unit Credit Cost Method – Under this funding method, the normal cost of each individual's pension is calculated as the cost for the accrual occurring in that year. Pay is projected to the member's retirement age.

R

Real Estate Investment Trust (REIT) – A REIT is a company that owns, operates or finances income-producing real estate.

Risk-Free Rate – The theoretical rate of return of an investment with zero risk. The risk-free rate represents the interest an investor would expect from an absolutely risk-free investment over a specified period of time.

Risk Premium – The return in excess of the risk-free rate of return an investment is expected to yield. An asset's risk premium is a form of compensation for investors who tolerate the extra risk, compared to that of a risk-free asset.

S

Smoothing – Used in developing the actuarial value of assets, smoothing is a technique employed by actuaries to minimize random variations in asset returns. This method shows the underlying trends in the asset values.

T

Target Asset Allocation – A component of a pension plan's investment policy. A target allocation exists for each asset class.

Treasury Inflation Protected Securities (TIPS) – This type of investment provides protection against inflation. The principal of a TIPS increases with inflation and decreases with deflation, as measured by the Consumer Price Index. When a TIPS matures, the investor is paid the adjusted principal or original principal, whichever is greater.

U

Unfunded Accrued Liability (UAL) – The difference between the accrued liability and the trust's assets.

V

Volatility – The amount of uncertainty or risk about the size of changes in a security's value. A higher volatility means a security's value can potentially be spread out over a larger range of values.

Z

Zero Coupon Bond – A bond that is issued at a deep discount to its face value and pays no interest.